who knew?

the best of
vol. 1 & 2

who knew?

the best of
vol. 1 & 2

Bruce Lubin & Jeanne Bossolina Lubin

CASTLE POINT PUBLISHING

Cover design: Richard Pasquarelli

Interior design: Christine Heun

Composed by Quadrum Solutions Pvt. Ltd.

Castle Point Publishing

58 Ninth Street

Hoboken, NJ 07030

ISBN: 978-0-9820667-6-8

Printed and bound in the United States of America

10 9 8 7 6 5 4 3 2 1

Please note: While this compilation of hints and tips will solve many of your household problems, total success cannot be guaranteed. The authors have compiled the information contained herein from a variety of sources, and neither the authors, publisher, manufacturer, nor distributor can assume responsibility for the effectiveness of the suggestions. Caution is urged when using any of the solutions, recipes, or tips in this book. At press time, all internet addresses and offers were valid and in working order; however, Castle Point Publishing is not responsible for the content of these sites, and no warranty or representation is made by Castle Point Publishing in regards to them or the outcome of any of the solicitations, solutions, recipes, or tips herein. Castle Point Publishing shall have no liability for damages (whether direct, indirect, consequential or otherwise) arising from the use, attempted use, misuse, or application of any of the solutions, recipes, or tips described in this book.

Dedication

For Jack, Terrence, and Aidan, as always

Acknowledgments

We're grateful to our families and friends for putting up with us while we wrote this book, and offering help and suggestions that were greatly appreciated. Thanks to Brian Scevola, who first suggested we start writing down all of our household know-how, and to Joy Mangano, whose support we will be forever grateful for. Thank-you to Karen Matsu Greenberg for her energy and unsurpassed production wisdom, Jennifer Boudinot for performing miracles and not minding the PATH train, Richard Pasquarelli for his talent and generosity, and Christine Heun for her beautiful designs. Also thanks to Joanie Rudolph and Andrea Cajuste, who showed us around the frightening world of logistics and shipping; Beth Blackburn and Maureen Lordon, for keeping our engines running; and Rizwan Burji, Jatin Mehta, and everyone at Quadrum Solutions for doing a remarkable job, even though our manuscript is always late. Finally, a big thank-you to all of our friends and fans who have given us tips through email and our website, WhoKnewTips.com. We couldn't do it without you!

Contents

PART ONE

All Around
the House
and Garden

Saving money starts at home, and the tips in this section will give you simple, easy ways to make your money go further in every room of your house (and in the garden, too). As you move from room to room, discover how to clean your home using all-natural, homemade cleaners, get rid of any kind of stain on the planet, and easily paint and perform household repairs. Outside, we'll tell you how to get rid of pests that invade your garden using ingredients you already have, easily take care of your plants, and keep your home looking as beautiful on the outside as it is on the inside. Whether you're a novice at saving money or you consider yourself scrimping royalty, you're bound to find lots of tricks that will have you saying, "Who knew?"

CHAPTER 1

Your Living Room

Minimize Broom-Swept Dust

The trail of dust that your broom leaves behind can be eliminated: Just fill a spray bottle with three parts water and one part liquid fabric softener, and spray the broom before sweeping. The spritz makes the broom strands more pliable, and helps it collect dirt more efficiently.

Quick Dusting

Instead of using a rag, wear a pair of old socks on your hands when dusting. It's efficient (you're using both hands), cheap (remember, these are old socks), and you can wash and reuse them, too.

Get a Lampshade Dust Free

The trick to cleaning a pleated lampshade is finding the right tool. Stroke each pleat from top to bottom with a dry, clean paintbrush. Or use a rolling lint remover for a quicker clean.

Forget that Pricey Dust Cloth, Make Your Own!

Don't bother buying fancy dust cloths that are treated to attract dust. Instead, simply sprinkle a piece of cheesecloth with a few drops of lemon oil. Let the cheesecloth air dry, and it will do just as good a job as an expensive cloth.

A DIY Duster for Hard-to-Reach Spots

Wrap a paper towel around the broad end of a kitchen spatula and secure with a rubber band. Use this to reach dust trapped between tubes of a radiator. Spray the paper towel with all-purpose cleaner to get rid of sticky spills and stains.

Another great use for a used fabric softener sheet? Run it across the TV screen, which will not only clean off the dust, but eliminate static cling.

For a Shiny Chandelier

There's no need to buy special chandelier cleaners. When it's time to tackle this difficult job, use a cloth dripping with a solution of two parts rubbing alcohol and one part hot water. Just slop it on, and be sure to hang an umbrella upside down from the chandelier to catch the mess.

The Art of Hanging

To hang lightweight artwork that's not in a heavy frame, there's no need to buy picture wire. Dental floss will do the trick.

Bookshelf Decorating Done Easily

A pair of wine bottles, either full or empty, makes great bookends for your shelf—especially if there are cookbooks on it!

Got Old, Smelly Books?

If your books stink, try this tactic for wiping out mildew. Dust mildewed pages with corn flour, French chalk, or talcum powder. Leave it inside the closed book for several days, then brush it off.

Out of Furniture Polish? Check the Pantry!

Vegetable oil works wonderfully on wood furniture. A very light coat will nourish the wood and help protect the finish, but be sure to rub it in well so it doesn't leave a residue. Leftover brewed tea (at room temp) can also be used on wood furniture.

Keep Wood Wonderful

Preserve the beauty of wood by rubbing the surface with boiled linseed oil. Wipe away the excess with a soft cloth.

Prevent Sun Stroke on Wood Furniture

Don't keep your good wood furniture in direct sunlight, especially during the hot summer. It damages the finish and can bleach the wood.

Who Knew? Readers' Favorite

Stale beer is a great cleanser for wooden furniture. Dampen a soft, clean cloth, wipe it on, and follow by wiping with a dry cloth.

Prevent Polish Buildup

Excess polish can build up and leave a dull finish on wooden furniture. To remove it, mix together 2 tablespoons white vinegar and 2 tablespoons water. Apply to the surface and wipe off at once. Alternatively, cornstarch will also do the trick: Sprinkle a little on the furniture and polish with a soft cloth.

Mask Scratches in Wood Furniture

If you notice a scratch, try this crafty (and delicious!) solution. Find a nut that matches the color of the wood; the most common types for this purpose are pecans, walnuts, and hazelnuts. Rub the scratched area gently with the broken edges of the nuts—using the insides, not the shells. When you're all done, enjoy a snack break.

Another Prescription for Scratches

Repair scratches in your wood furniture with shoe polish. A crayon also works. Just find a color that's a close match to the wood, then rub the crayon or polish into the scratch. Wipe off any excess wax with a credit card edge, then buff with a cotton cloth.

Say "Vamoose" to Water Stains on Wood

Does your wood furniture have white rings left from wet glasses? Remove them with a mixture of 2 tablespoons corn oil and enough salt to make a paste. Apply the paste to the rings and let stand for at least one hour before rubbing the area gently. If the finish on your furniture is very delicate, you can substitute baking soda for the salt (it's less abrasive). If neither of those mixtures works, give mayonnaise a shot: Rub a tiny bit (½ teaspoon) on the ring with a paper towel and let it sit overnight. In the morning, just wipe with a damp cloth and the ring should be gone!

Surprising Furniture Fix

If you have a mark on your wood furniture or floor that won't come off with furniture polish, try leaving mayonnaise (yes, mayonnaise!) on the stain for an hour, then wiping off.

A Cheaper Cushion

You've probably seen those little cushions with the sticky material on the back that can be placed on the bottom of furniture or the backs of picture frames to keep them from scratching. Rather than spending the money for these expensive items, buy cushions for corns and bunions instead! As long as they aren't medicated, they're the exact same thing, and usually much cheaper.

Slipcover Secret

When washing a slipcover for a couch or chair, put it back on your furniture while the cover is still damp. Not only will the slipcover be easier to get on, but it won't need to be ironed. It will help keep them from shrinking, too!

Need More Storage Space?

If your living room sofa has a skirt that reaches the floor, you have storage space you didn't even know of. Underneath the sofa is a great place to store a bin of wrapping paper and accessories, old photo albums, and other skinny items you reach for often.

A Clean Home for Your Fish

The easiest way to clean a fish bowl is to wipe the inside with a cloth soaked in white vinegar, which will help remove mineral deposits. Just make sure you rinse the bowl thoroughly before putting your fish back in.

Who Knew? Readers' Favorite

The easiest way to keep your dog or cat off of your good furniture when you're out is to place a piece of aluminum foil on it. They hate the feeling under their paws, and will stay way.

Cure for Cat Clawing

Here's something you probably didn't know: Cats hate hot sauce. So if you can't get your cat to stop clawing at your woodwork, just rub in a little hot sauce, buff it thoroughly, and your cat will stay clear.

Easily Clean Up Pet Hair

Pet hair all over the house? The easiest way to clean it up is to rub the furniture, carpet, or any other shedding victims (including the pet himself!) with a fresh dryer sheet.

Another Quick Pet Hair Remover

Uh oh, guests are on their way and you've just realized that your beloved cat has made a cat-fur nest all over your couch. For a quick and easy way to remove pet hair from furniture, turn to your rubber dishwashing gloves. Just slip them on, then rub the offending furniture with them. The hair will stick to the gloves and you can quickly throw it away.

Quick Fix for Messy Paws

Forget about using soap and water on your dog's messy paws. It's faster and easier to simply wipe his paws with a baby wipe. It's a great way to remove dirt and mud—before he cuddles up with you on the couch.

Who Knew? Readers' Favorite

To keep votive candles from sticking to their holders after a night of wax run-off, add a little sand or water to the bottom of the holder before you light the candle. This will keep the wax from making a mess at the bottom.

Sponge off Candle Soot

If your beautiful candle is staining your walls with black soot marks, don't try to simply scrub them away—that'll only make more of a mess. Instead, remove those unsightly spots by sponging them with rubbing alcohol.

Slow and Steady with the Heat

When it's time to turn on the heat, be patient. Your house won't heat up any faster if you crank the thermostat way up, but you *are* likely to forget to turn it down, which can be a huge energy waster.

A Ceiling Fan Can Keep You Warm Too

Don't let your fan go to waste just because it's no longer warm outside. To stay toasty during the frigid days of winter, hit the reverse switch to push hot air down into your room.

Homemade Air Fresheners

You don't have to spend hard-earned cash to keep your house smelling nice. Freshen it up with these crafty odor-fighting tricks.

✦ Make a great homemade air freshener with an orange: Just cut the orange in half, remove the pulp, and fill with salt. It's effective, easy—and cheap!

✦ If you're not a great baker, but love the smell of fresh baked goods, try this trick: Dab a few drops of vanilla extract on a cool light bulb, then turn it on. When it heats up, the room will be filled with a wonderful smell.

✦ To keep the house smelling fresh during the dog days of summer, tape fabric softener sheets onto your air conditioner filter, under the grate. Not only will it exude a lovely smell, but it also makes the filter last longer.

Refresh Potpourri

If your favorite potpourri loses its scent, it's easy to revive—with vodka. Yep, you read that right. Just pour a little vodka into a spray bottle and spritz the potpourri, mixing it up so each piece is saturated.

Stop Smoky Smells

Did you know that a bowl of sliced apples will remove the smell of cigarette smoke in an enclosed space? The next time you have a smoky party, cut up some apples and leave them around the house before you go to bed.

Vacuum Off Odors

To rid your house of pet, cooking, or other smells, add a cotton ball soaked in vanilla or lavender oil to your vacuum cleaner bag, and vacuum away. It's a great way to rid your home of an offensive odor by creating a nice scent instead.

Soak Up the Water in Your Umbrella Stand

Water can collect in umbrella stands. Prevent this by cutting a large sponge to fit in the bottom. Remove it and wring it out as necessary.

Feed Plants from Your Fish Tank

If you have an aquarium, save the water each time you change it and use it to water your houseplants. The fishy water contains nitrogen, potassium, and phosphorus—all three function as natural fertilizers for plants. You'll be amazed at the results.

There Really Is a Use for Dryer Lint!

Use dryer lint to prevent dirt from falling out of your potted houseplants when you water them: Place some dryer lint in the pots so it covers the holes. The water will drain out, but the dirt will stay in!

Clean Up Sooty Bricks with Cola

Try an old masonry trick to brighten up soot-stained brick. Mix a can of cola with 3½ fluid ounces all-purpose household cleaner and 7 pints water in a bucket. Sponge onto sooty brick and leave for 15 minutes. Loosen the soot by scrubbing with a stiff-bristled brush. Sponge with clean water. For a stronger solution, add more cola.

Candle Scandal

Removing candle wax from your wood floors is easy if you soften the wax first with a blow dryer, then peel off. Wipe any excess with a paper towel, and then clean with a mixture of half white vinegar and half water.

⬤ Who Knew?

According to a recent study, many paraffin-based candles emit toxic fumes. If you have asthma, allergies, or respiratory problems, you may want to go with a soy-based candle instead.

Drop a Glass? Sacrifice a Sandwich

If your post–New Year's Eve clean-up involves collecting the shattered remains of Champagne glasses—or if you've merely dropped a glass on the floor—try out this crafty tip. Dampen a piece of white bread, and dab on the glass fragments. It's much more effective than using a broom.

Get Gleaming Wood Floors

There's no need to buy a special cleaner for your wood floors. Simply mix equal parts vegetable oil and white vinegar in a spray bottle, and apply. Then shine with a clean cloth until the solution is gone.

Patch Up Carpet Burns

Here's how to eliminate cigarette burns in your carpet: First, cut away the burn mark. Then, cut a bit of carpet from an area that's covered by a piece of furniture (e.g., under a couch), and glue it carefully over the burnt spot. Finally, smack the person who dropped the ashes.

Salt Does the Trick on Carpet Stains

If you spill red wine or anything else with a bright pigment on your carpet, pour salt on the area as soon as possible and watch it absorb the wine almost instantly. Wait until it dries, then vacuum it up. Salt tends to provide a special capillary attraction that will work for most liquids. Baking soda, with its high sodium content, works with wine too. Salt also works on mud stains.

Remove Pen Marks from Leather

If your kid has decided to write a novel on your favorite leather chair, don't panic. Just blot the stain with milk until the ink disappears, then wipe it clean with a damp sponge.

A great way to clean wallpaper is with white bread. You can eliminate fingerprints, light stains, and even ball point ink by simply rubbing a piece of white bread vigorously over the spot.

Spruce Up Satin and Gloss Finishes

Clean painted walls with a solution made of 4 fluid ounces white vinegar, 1 ounce washing soda, and 1 pint water. Or, mix 7 ounces ammonia, 1 teaspoon dish soap, and 7 pints water.

Longer-Lasting Blooms

There are quite a few ways to prolong the life of fresh flowers. First, change the water and trim the stems every day. Instead of water, use a solution of 2 tablespoons white vinegar and 2 tablespoons sugar in a quart of water—or add ½ cup baking soda to a quart of water. If you have roses, crush the stems at the ends to encourage absorption of water. If you have tulips, make a series of small holes down the length of their stems with a pin instead. And if you're displaying carnations, place them in carbonated lemonade (not the diet variety) rather than water. Change every four days.

Keep Your Overpriced Flowers Fresh

Florists sometimes cut flowers in the open air, which allows air into the stems and prevents the flowers from absorbing all the water they need. To ensure that your store-bought flowers stay fresh longer, submerge the stems in hot water, and trim an inch off the ends.

Vinegar for Vases

Don't put a beautiful bouquet of flowers in a cloudy vase! To make it shine like new, just pour a little white vinegar and uncooked rice inside, swish it around, and watch the clouds disappear.

Flower Arranging Done Easily

When arranging flowers, use transparent tape across the mouth of the vase in a grid to make an invisible guide. Not only will it be easier to decide where to put each flower, but they'll stay more upright with the tape to lean against.

Who Knew?

You may have heard the old household tip about extending the life of your cut flowers by adding a penny to the bottom of the vase. However, today's pennies aren't made with enough copper to effectively work as a fungicide. Pennies made before 1981 do, however, so if you find one, make sure to keep it for your flowers.

The Way to Water

Try watering your houseplants with ice cubes. That way, the water won't run straight through the plant, and you'll avoid a muddy mess.

Shinier, Prettier Plants

If your houseplants are dusty, gently wipe the leaves with a soft cloth and a damp sponge. If you want your plants' leaves to *really* shine, rub them (gently!) with a cotton ball dipped in either mayonnaise, diluted mineral oil, or a solution of half baking soda and half water. Wipe off any excess with a soft cloth.

Got Stale Milk? Use It!

Stale milk will do a great job of cleaning plant leaves. The protein in milk called "casein" has a mild cleansing effect on the plant cell walls.

Clay Flowerpot Caveat

Never place a clay pot on wooden furniture, unless you use a coaster. Clay is porous, so water will seep through and possibly damage the wood finish.

● Who Knew?

Daffodils are one of our favorite flowers. Just remember not to mix them with other flowers when making an arrangement, as daffodils produce a toxin that kills other flowers!

Put Your Plants on Autopilot While You're Away

If you are going on a long vacation and are unable to find someone to care for your plants, try either of these clever watering techniques.

✦ Place a large container of water near your plant (if you have several, gather them into one spot to make it easy). Then place one end of a long piece of yarn into the water, and stick the other end into the plant's soil, near the roots.

Lay the strand across the stalks of the plant. This will keep it moist until you return.

✦ Poke a small hole in the side of a plastic bottle, fill it with water, and place it in the soil next to your plant. The slow drip keeps the plants watered slowly but continuously.

Plants Love Starch

Your houseplants need nourishment, particularly in the dead of winter when the sunlight is limited, yet there's no need to buy expensive plant food. Just remember to save the water in which you boil potatoes or pasta, let it cool, and use it to water your plants. They love the starchy water.

Protect Your Soil (and Your Shirt!)

To keep mud from spattering when you water plants in window boxes, top the soil with a half-inch layer of gravel. Do the same for outdoor plants to prevent mud bombs during heavy rainfalls.

Grease Up Your Windows

Don't pull a muscle trying to shove open a stuck heavy window. Windows will open and close more easily if you occasionally rub a bar of soap across the track.

Cleaning Aluminum Blinds

Aluminum blinds are great for keeping out light, but they can be hard to clean! The easiest way to clean smudges off aluminum blinds is with a pencil eraser. Dust will come off with a few swipes of a fabric softener sheet.

You don't need expensive cleaners to wash your windows! For a cheap, effective glass cleaner, fill a spray bottle with ½ teaspoon dishwashing liquid, 3 tablespoons white vinegar, and 2 cups warm water. If you're washing something that's very dirty, use more liquid soap.

Window Washing 101

If the sun is shining on your windows, wait until they are in the shade to wash them. When they dry too fast, they tend to streak.

Dusting Your Blinds

Is there any chore more annoying than dusting your Venetian blinds? Luckily, you don't have to buy one of those "blinds cleaners" found in stores. Instead, use bread crusts. Just hold a piece of crust around each slat, then run it along the length of the blinds. An old paintbrush will also do the trick, or use the brush attachment on your vacuum cleaner.

Quickly Clean Mini-Blinds

Give mini-blinds a good clean by simply throwing them in the bathtub filled with water and white vinegar, or your favorite cleanser. Just give them a good shake, and hang them up wet. There may be a few streaks once they've air-dried, but they're nearly impossible to spot.

For Cleaner Shades

Stubborn smudges and stains on your window shades? Lay the shades on a table or countertop and rub the spots with an art-gum eraser (which can be found at art or office supply stores). It will erase the smudges away!

Tip for Hanging Curtains

When slipping curtains over a metal rod, first place a plastic freezer or sandwich bag over the metal end. This will help you avoid snagging the curtains so they go on easily.

CHAPTER 2

The Kitchen and Dining Room

Warm-Weather Dishwasher Tip

Here's a terrific tip to use during warm weather: Turn off your dishwasher after the rinse cycle is done, open it up, and let your dishes drip-dry. You'll save a lot by avoiding the heat-drying cycle on your machine.

Ease Your Energy Bill

Even when you're not using appliances, they still continue to use energy. So pull the plug when you're done with the blender, toaster, food processor, even your television—everything except appliances that need constant power to preserve a special setting.

Energy Saving Tips for Your Fridge

Clean the condenser coils on the back of your refrigerator twice a year, and you'll use less energy while increasing the life of the appliance as well. It's important also to keep your freezer packed—even with bags of ice blocks if necessary—because a full freezer in much more efficient than one which is half empty.

The Ice Trick

When you go away on vacation, fill a sealable plastic bag with a few ice cubes and put it in the freezer. If a power failure occurs while you are away, the ice will melt and refreeze in a solid block, alerting you that your frozen food has been defrosted.

Set Up an Efficient Kitchen

Organize your kitchen so your hot appliances (an oven or dishwasher) don't sit near your cold appliances (the fridge). They'll have to work harder to do their jobs. Also, make sure your refrigerator isn't exposed to direct sunlight or heat vents. These simple tips will help keep your kitchen in tip-top shape and your energy costs down.

Battery Booster

Batteries will last longer if they're stored in the refrigerator. To boost their energy, place them in the sun for a day before you use them.

Microwave Safety

Microwave doors may become misaligned, especially if you pull down on them when opening them. When the doors don't close properly, they can leak radiation, making your food take longer to cook. Check them periodically with a small, inexpensive detector, which can be purchased in any hardware store.

Thrifty Kitchen Storage

Save space by reusing an empty six-pack holder to store aluminum foil, plastic wrap, waxed paper, and other boxes of wrap. Stand the long boxes on their ends, insert them into the plastic rings, and put them under your sink. This'll free up a valuable kitchen drawer.

A Pantry Pointer

Keep packets of sauces and gravies in one easy-to-manage spot in your pantry—we suggest using an empty child's shoebox! Stand the envelopes upright in the box, so the labels are easy to read, and the shoebox should fit perfectly on a shelf in your pantry.

When you're preparing a big meal and need more counter space, try this clever quick fix: Simply open a drawer in your kitchen and cover it with a heavy-duty cutting board. Voilà!

Organize with Vases

Put all those vases you get with flower bouquets to good use. Use them on your kitchen counter to store gadgets, large utensils, or anything else that is clogging up your drawers.

Free Up Shelf Space with Hanging Cup Storage

Under-the-shelf cup holders are a clever, super-efficient way to save space in your kitchen. You can buy a slip-on cup holder for less than $10, no tools required. You'll save tons of shelf space for plates and bowls, while your cups, mugs, glasses, and cooking utensils stay out of the way.

A System for All Those Plastic Lids

Are plastic lids taking over your kitchen? We feel your pain, and can offer a solution: Store a dish drainer in your cabinet, and file the lids on their sides in size order. You'll find the lid you need in seconds, and your kitchen will seem much more organized.

For a No-Scratch Stack

Stacking fine china? Insert paper plates between the real plates before stacking to prevent scratches.

Storing Knives

Two of the best places to store knives are on a magnetic rack or in a wooden countertop knife block. Never store knives in a drawer with other utensils. Not only do you risk injury, but the knife blades may become nicked and dented.

Raise a Glass

To prevent glasses from becoming dusty, place them upside down on shelves. Arrange in order of size so they are easier to find and also to avoid breakages.

How to Store Those Plastic Bags

Plastic grocery bags have a way of multiplying and taking over kitchen drawers. A space-saving solution is to stuff all of them into an empty tissues box. You'll be amazed how many fit, and you can easily remove them one at a time when you need to.

Clean a Dusty Dust Mop

Always clean dust mops after using them. To avoid making a dust cloud, cover a dry dust mop with a damp paper bag before you shake it out. If your mop has a removable head, put it in a large mesh lingerie bag and toss it into the washer.

Naturally Deodorize Garbage Cans

Wash and deodorize trash cans with a solution of 1 teaspoon lemon juice mixed with 1 quart water. Sprinkling baking soda into the base of every garbage bag will also help keep odors at bay.

There's no need to throw out your stinky, old sponges. Just soak them in cold salt water, rinse, and they're good to use again.

Odor Eaters

All sorts of nasty odors lurk in the kitchen, whether it's expired food, a lingering trash bag, or a mix of flavors still hanging around after a meal. Next time you've got a persistent stink, try out one of these quickie odor-killing tips.

✦ Keep a few washed charcoal briquettes in a shallow dish on top of the refrigerator.

✦ To eliminate refrigerator odors, leave a small cup of fresh coffee grounds on two shelves.

✦ Deep-fry a small amount of cinnamon to chase all odors from your home.

Make Your Home Smell Sugar-and-Spice Nice

For a great DIY home fragrance, simmer apple cider with a cinnamon stick and a few whole cloves. Also add a bit of orange peel, if you like. Isn't this what Martha Stewart smells like?

Freshen Up the Garbage Disposal

Keep your garbage disposal running properly and odor-free with this simple once-a-month trick: Grind about a dozen ice cubes made from white vinegar. The ice sharpens the blades while the vinegar deodorizes the drain.

Quick Fix for a Stinky Microwave

Microwave odors? Cut a lemon in quarters and put it in a bowl of water, then put in the microwave on high for 2 minutes. As long as the bowl is oven-safe, this will work for oven odors, too (just keep it in for longer).

Orange Oven

A self-cleaning oven can leave an odor after it's done its work. Eliminate the lingering smell by turning down the oven to 350° when it's finished, then putting orange peels on a baking sheet inside. Let the oven cook the peels for half an hour, and not only will the oven smell fresh, but your whole kitchen will, too!

Admit It, Your Fridge Sometimes Smells

Besides baking soda, a number of other foods are capable of removing odors. Pour a little vanilla extract into a bottle cap and set in the refrigerator to absorb odors. One of the best ways to eliminate odors from your refrigerator is to hollow out a grapefruit or orange and fill it with salt, and place in the back of the fridge. Leave it there until the salt gets completely damp, and then throw the whole thing out and replace.

Time to Clean Out Your Refrigerator?

When cleaning your refrigerator, don't use chemicals that can linger on your food and produce nasty odors. After emptying the fridge, simply dissolve a cup of salt in a gallon of hot water and wipe away. Squeeze in the juice of a lemon for a nice scent.

Spruce Up Your Stainless Steel Sink

Nothing makes a kitchen look better than a shiny kitchen sink, and luckily, there are a lot of ways to clean and shine stainless steel!

✦ Club soda is a terrific way to clean stainless steel sinks, dishwashers, ranges, and other appliances. The least expensive club soda works as well as the pricey brands; and flat club soda works too. Add a little flour for really stubborn stains.

✦ Stainless steel can also be quickly and easily cleaned with vodka. Place a little on a sponge or paper towel and wipe. Your faucet, sink, and other stainless steel will soon be sparkling again, so pour yourself a little glass to celebrate!

✦ Instead of using a rag or a paper towel, use newspaper, which will get it even shinier. A tougher option is aluminum foil. Just crumple it up, and scour with the shiny side.

✦ For a spectacularly shiny finish on a stainless steel or aluminum sink, rub a liberal amount of baking soda in a circular motion all over its surface with a damp sponge.

✦ For the shiniest sink you've ever seen, finish off your cleaning session by buffing the sink to a sleek shine with a touch of baby oil on a soft cloth.

Oven Cleaning Made Easy

A simple way to clean your oven is to place an oven-safe pot or bowl filled with water inside. Heat on 450° for 20 minutes to loosen dirt and grease with the steam. Once your oven is cool, wipe off the condensation and the grease will come with it. After you're done, make a paste of water and baking soda and smear it on any enamel. The paste will dry into a protective layer that will absorb grease as you cook.

Not a Fan of Oven Fans?

Oven fans are magnets for grease. The simplest way to clean the resulting mess is to pop out the fan filter, then run it through your dishwasher on the top shelf.

Who Knew?

Most aerosol oven cleaners contain lye, also found in drain cleaners. When you spray lye on burned fats and carbohydrates, it converts them to soap that can be wiped off with a damp cloth. While this works well for cleaning, lye is a powerful chemical that's very toxic. If possible, choose one of the newer oven cleaners that use organic salts— they're less noxious. Whichever type you use, make sure that your kitchen is well ventilated or the cleaner fumes can burn the lining of your mouth and throat.

De-Gunk Your Can Opener

To clean your electric can opener, run a piece of paper towel or waxed paper through it. This will pick up the grease and some of the gunk.

Clean Your Coffee Maker

For the best tasting coffee, make sure to clean your coffee maker regularly. Just add several tablespoons of baking soda to your pot, fill it with water, and then run your coffee maker as usual. It's a good idea to run it again with just water. You can also use a denture-cleaning tablet instead of baking soda.

Now Clean Your Coffee Grinder!

Even your coffee grinder needs a good clean every now and then, and uncooked rice can do the job. Simply mill a handful of rice as you normally do to your coffee beans. The chopped rice cleans out the stuck coffee grounds and oils, and absorbs the stale odors to boot. Afterwards, throw away the rice, wipe the grinder clean...and brew fresh coffee.

Lube Up Your Blender

To keep your blender and mixer in top working order, be sure to lubricate all moving parts with a very light coating of mineral oil (*not* vegetable oil). This should be done every three months.

Getting Rid of Counter Stains

Stubborn stains can be removed from your countertop by applying a baking soda paste and rubbing with a warm, damp cloth. If the stain still remains, consider using a drop or two of bleach, but be careful: Bleach can fade your countertop along with the stain!

Cease Grease!

Forget about buying those expensive stove cleaners to get rid of cooked-on grease stains. Just wet the stains with vinegar and cover with baking soda. After watching the fun, foaming reaction, wipe with a damp sponge and buff with a dry, clean cloth.

Make a Gross Chore Easier

Eventually, it's time for our worst cleaning chores. After you tackle the top of your grimy fridge (using vinegar usually does the trick), place an old placemat on top. When it gets gross, either replace it or throw it in the washing machine for a quick clean.

Who Knew?

It may be a chore, but cleaning the dust and debris from behind your refrigerator will help it run more efficiently and save money on electricity, too.

Enamel Enhancers

Remove stains from enamel with a paste of baking soda and hydrogen peroxide. It will form a gentle bleach that you can rub in and leave to dry, then rinse off.

Cut Grease with Ammonia

Ammonia is a no-nonsense cleaning essential for your kitchen. To clean a really greasy pan, add a few drops of ammonia into your soapsuds.

Great All-Purpose Cleaner

For a perfect all-purpose cleaner, mix together 1 gallon hot water, 3½ fluid ounces ammonia, 3½ fluid ounces white vinegar, and 7 ounces (1¼ cups) baking soda together. Store in a tightly sealed bottle and use on glass, silver, and countertops.

Perk Up Your Floor

If you have black scuff marks on your linoleum or vinyl flooring, you can remove them with a bit of white (not gel) toothpaste. Simply rub the toothpaste over the scuff vigorously until it disappears.

Make Your Ceramic Floors Gleam

There are tons of commercial cleaning products for ceramic floors, but they're costly, toxic, and liable to irritate your skin. Luckily, they can be easily replaced with this safe homemade alternative: Combine 1 cup white vinegar and 1 gallon warm water, and mop till those floors sparkle.

Vinegar as Floor Cleaner

For mopping vinyl floors, use ½ cup white vinegar added to 1 gallon warm water. It's cheap, effective, and completely non-toxic.

Who Knew? Readers' Favorite

If your vinyl tile has loosened, simply put it back in its original place, lay a piece of aluminum foil on top, and run a hot iron over it. In no time at all, the glue will begin to adhere. Then just stack a few books on top of the tile until the glue hardens again.

Shiny Chrome

What is chrome for, if not to be shiny? To bring back dull chrome fixtures, dampen them, then rub them with newspaper. You can also shine them up with a paste of vinegar and cream of tartar.

For the Best Potholders

Even your potholders don't have to look stained and dirty. Wash frequently, and after each time you wash them, spray them with starch. Spray starch repels grease, so your potholders will stay unstained.

Conserve Steel-Wool Pads

It's easy to keep your wet, soaped steel-wool pads from rusting: Just wrap them in aluminum foil and store in your freezer. But before you do, cut them in half before using them. It's economical, because they won't wear out as fast and keeps half rust-free. And as a bonus, it's a great way to sharpen your scissors.

Handle with Care

If you've ever experienced the frustration of breaking a dish while cleaning it, you'll love this tip! Prevent breakages by lining your sink with a towel or rubber mat before washing.

Who Knew? Readers' Favorite

There's no need to buy expensive dishwashing liquid. Buy the cheapest brand you can find, then add a few tablespoons of white vinegar to the water while you're washing, and your dishes will shine. The same is true for dishwashers—just buy the least expensive detergent, and add in some white vinegar to the machine. Vinegar will remove spots from glass in a flash.

Stuck-On Substances

If you've given up hope of ever removing stuck-on food in your pots and pans, help is on the way—in the form of a fabric softener sheet! Just cover the stain with hot water, and float a fabric softener sheet in it. Leave overnight, and in the morning, the food should wipe off easily.

Cast Iron Cure

The best way to clean cast iron pans is to cover any stain with a paste of cream of tartar and white vinegar. Apply liberally, let it sit, then scrub with a damp, soft cloth.

What if Your Nonstick Pan Sticks?

For the most part, coated pots and pans are easy to keep clean, but they do stain, and over time grease and oil may build up. This will adversely affect the efficiency of the nonstick surface, so it's important to clean and re-season any stained areas. To do so, simply mix 1 cup water, 2 tablespoons baking soda, and ½ cup white vinegar in the pot, set on the stove, and boil for 10 minutes. Wash the pot as usual, then rub vegetable oil on the surface of the plastic coating to re-season it.

Burnt Food Be Gone

Here's another great way to remove burnt food from pans. Sprinkle baking soda, salt, and dishwasher detergent over the crusty bits, then cover with water and boil for a half an hour. Even the toughest baked-on food will wipe off easily.

For a Sparkling Coffee Pot

To remove coffee stains from inside of a glass coffee pot, add 1 tablespoon water, 4 teaspoons salt, and 1 cup crushed ice. Gently swirl until it is clean, then rinse thoroughly. (Just make sure the coffee pot is at room temperature before cleaning.)

Get Rid of a Smelly Thermos

The easiest way to remove smells and stains from a thermos is by filling it with hot water and ½ cup baking soda, then letting it sit overnight. In the morning, just rinse well, and it should be good as new!

Remove Stubborn Stains

Get rid of really tough stains on your metal and ceramic pots, pans, mugs, and dishes by filling them with boiling water and adding a denture tablet. Let it sit overnight, and the stain should disappear.

This Cup Has Seen a Lot of Coffee!

If the inside of your coffee cup is stained from coffee or tea, it's not too late to get it to look like new. Mix a paste of coarse salt (or baking soda) and water. Scrub the mug with this, then rinse well.

Who Knew? Readers' Favorite

Cleaning a cheese grater will never be a problem if you grate a small piece of raw potato before trying to wash it out. Sometimes an old toothbrush also comes in handy for cleaning graters.

Crystal Clean

Use a paste of lemon juice and baking powder to remove small stains from crystal. Treat tougher stains by placing 2 teaspoons uncooked rice inside the crystal piece, adding water, and swirling. The small amount of abrasive action from the rice will remove the stains—perfect for vases with narrow necks.

Camouflage a Crack in Your China

Antique dealers use this trick to hide hairline cracks on china plates and cups. Simmer the piece in milk for 45 minutes. Casein, a milk protein, may fill in the crack, depending on its size. If your china is old or fragile, though, this could backfire—heat can cause pieces to expand and crack.

Nix the Nicks

Buff away a nick on the rim of a glass or your china with an emery board. Don't use a nail file or sandpaper; both are too coarse and will scratch the glass.

Everything You Need to Know to Care for Your Silver

If you didn't get it as a wedding present, you probably have silver cutlery that has been passed down from generation to generation. This beautiful silverware is always a nice treat on a special occasion. But as you've probably discovered, silver will eventually tarnish if exposed to air for an extended period of time, turning duller and darker as time goes on. However, you can keep your silver shiny and beautiful by polishing and storing it wisely.

✦ Never combine silver and stainless steel cutlery in the dishwasher—the silver will turn black. Any contact with dishwasher detergent will also result in black spots. Remove silver cutlery from the dishwasher immediately after the cycle ends, and dry at once to avoid stains and pitting from salt residue.

✦ Sulfur compounds in the air cause silver to tarnish; to prevent this, store your silver in airtight containers, or wrap it in tarnish-proof cloths or papers. (Never wrap silver in plastic food wrap. It will keep air away, but it can also cause stains and corrosion.)

✦ If your silver does develop spots, dissolve a little salt in lemon juice, then dip a soft cloth into the mixture and rub it onto the cutlery. Rinse in warm water and finish by buffing to a shine with a chamois.

✦ You can also rub off tarnish with toothpaste. Place some white (non-gel) toothpaste on a soft cloth and use it to rub solid silver (not silver plate). Then rinse it off gently. Don't use whitening toothpaste—it can damage the surface.

✦ To remove tarnish from the tines of a fork, coat a piece of cotton string with the toothpaste and run it between the tines.

✦ Polishing silver is never a neat chore, but an old sock can make it easier. Slip the sock over your hand; use one side to apply the polish and the other to buff it out.

✦ If you have large silver items that are not used with food, consider having them lacquered by a jeweler to prevent tarnishing. Candelabras, vases, and trophies are good candidates for this treatment.

✦ If you place a small piece of chalk in a silver chest, it will absorb moisture and slow tarnishing. Calcium carbonate (i.e., chalk) absorbs moisture from the air very slowly. Break up the chalk and expose the rough surface for the best results.

⬤ Who Knew?

In addition to being used for silverware and as a precious metal, silver is also used in electrical contacts and conductors, mirrors, and photographic film.

Copper Polisher

Believe it or not, a great way to polish copper is to rub it with ketchup and let it stand for an hour. Rinse off the ketchup with hot water, then buff to an incredible shine.

Lemon for Brass and Copper

One of the best cleaners for brass and copper is a simple lemon! Simply cut a lemon in half, sprinkle the cut side with salt, and rub over the surface you're cleaning. Rinse with cold water and watch it shine.

For Tablecloth Blunders

If you spill wine on a tablecloth, blot up as much as you can as soon as you can with a cloth, then sponge with cool water. Wash immediately. If the fabric is not machine washable, cover the stain with a small cloth dampened with a solution of detergent, water, and vinegar, then rinse. Get the cloth to the drycleaner as soon as you can.

Wax-Removing Wonder

Accidentally dripped candle wax on a tablecloth? Remove it by rubbing with an ice cube and then scraping with a dull knife. Another way to remove candle wax from a table or cloth is to place some brown paper (not newspaper) over the top and iron it on a low heat. The wax will transfer to the paper!

Keep Candleholders Clean

To prevent wax from sticking to a candleholder, rub a thin coat of olive oil on the base of the holder before lighting the candle. If your holder already has some wax buildup, mix olive oil with dish soap to clean it out.

Candlestick Fit

Most taper candles won't fit perfectly into standard candlesticks, so you'll have to do a little work to ensure your candle fits securely. (Do not light the candle and melt wax into the base—this is messy and dangerous!) First, try placing the candle base under hot water; this softens the wax and allows it to mold to its new surroundings. If this doesn't do the trick, whittle down the wax around the base of the candle with a paring knife, checking the fit as you go. Stop when you get it narrow enough to fit the holder. Apply wax adhesive around the base of the candle, and place it in the candlestick.

CHAPTER 3

The Bathroom

Bathroom Quick Clean

If you can only clean one room before guests arrive, make it the bathroom. It's the only room where your guests will be alone (and possibly snoop around!), and a dirty bathroom is worse than a cluttered living room. Here's how to do it in two minutes or less: Just apply a touch of baby shampoo to a wet sponge and wipe down your sink, fixtures, tiles, and bathtub. It cuts through oily residue, and smells good, too.

Steam Out a Nasty Bathroom

If you've let the bathroom get so dirty that it now resembles a gas station restroom, turn on the hot water in the shower for 10 minutes with the door closed. The steam will loosen the buildup of mildew and mold. Then, get in there and clean.

Mildew Remover

Looking for an easy mildew remover? Simply scrub the affected area with an old, damp toothbrush sprinkled with baking soda.

Ever-Useful Alcohol

Isopropyl alcohol, which is available at most grocery stores and pharmacies, is a cheap and effective disinfectant. But it also belongs in your bathroom cabinet for more than just first-aid purposes. Use it, mixed with equal parts water, to clean the bathtub caulking and shine chrome and glass.

Clogged Showerhead?

Removing mineral deposits from a showerhead without harsh chemicals is easy. Just unscrew it and submerge in white vinegar overnight, and the clogs disappear. If you can't unscrew it, fill a small, sturdy bag with vinegar and attach to the showerhead with duct tape. You can also brush the showerhead with vinegar using an old toothbrush to make it sparkle. To clean the screen in your showerhead, wash it with water with a dash of dishwashing liquid added.

Flour Power

If your chrome faucets are less than sparkly, try rubbing them with flour. Rinse, then buff with a soft cloth, and they'll really shine. Vinegar also works well for cleaning chrome.

Mirror Miracle

Make your mirrors shine with a solution of equal parts of vinegar and water. Use old newspapers to wipe the surface of mirrors with the mix, then add extra shine by rubbing with a clean dry-erase or blackboard eraser.

Who Knew?

Cleaning agents can leave a thin film on mirrors. Brighten mirrors by rubbing them with a cloth dampened with alcohol.

Get Rid of Copper Stains

Removing blue-green stains caused by high copper content in your water can be challenging, even with the help of bleach. Instead, treat the stains on your shower or tub with a paste of equal parts cream of tartar and baking soda. Rub into the stain, leave for half an hour, and rinse well with water. Repeat, if necessary.

Toilet Bowl Cleaner

To remove hard-water deposits in your toilet bowl, pour 1 cup white vinegar into the bowl and allow it to sit for several hours or overnight before scrubbing. A fizzy denture tablet works well, too!

Scouring Powder Substitute

The best thing about scouring powder is its abrasive action. The worst is the harsh chemical smell. Get all the benefits without the caustic chemicals by using baking soda instead. In most instances, baking soda will work just as well as scouring powder.

Soap Scum Solution

Clear soap scum away effortlessly from shower doors by wiping them with a used (dry) dryer sheet. It gets the job done quickly!

Spick-and-Span Shower Doors

Need to clean those dirty glass shower doors? You can wipe down the doors with leftover white wine (if you haven't finished it off!). Wipe the wine on with a damp sponge, leave for five minutes, then rinse off. Finish by quickly buffing with a clean, dry cloth.

Who Knew? Readers' Favorite

Need to remove mildew from a plastic shower curtain? Try washing the curtain in the washing machine with two large, white bath towels. Add a little bleach in with your usual detergent, and add 1 cup white vinegar to the rinse cycle to prevent future mildew growth.

Cleaning Your Shower Curtain

If your shower curtain has seen better days, wash according to the care label attached, but add a cup of vinegar to the water and it will look like new. Remove as soon as the cycle is complete and hang back in position to drip-dry without any creases.

Shower Curtain Savvy

Avoid leaving a shower curtain bunched up after use, especially in a small bathroom—the steam encourages mildew. Always close the shower curtain after use, and if small spots of mildew do appear, dab with baking soda on a damp cloth. Wash larger areas in hot detergent, rub with lemon juice, and dry in the sun, if possible.

Ceramic Care

To keep them sparkling, wipe ceramic tile regularly with a sponge damped with water and a splash of vinegar. Avoid soapy or oily cleaners and never use abrasives, which will dull the finish and make glazed tiles more prone to dirt.

Perfect Porcelain

Steel wool and scouring powders will scratch porcelain, so if your tub or sink is made of this fragile material, rub a freshly cut lemon around the surface to cut through grease, then rinse with running water.

Fabric Softener Sheets to the Rescue (Again)

To clean chrome-plated fixtures in your bathroom instantly, always keep fabric softener sheets handy. Just wipe, and the chrome will sparkle. Rubbing alcohol also does the trick.

Grout-Buster

If you've tried milder grout cleaners and you still have black stains on your grout, it's time to bring out the big boys. Make sure to wear protective gloves and that the area is well-ventilated, soak some paper towels in bleach and place them around the grout. Leave for at least an hour, then remove the towels and enjoy your clean, white grout.

Get Rid of Caked-On Hair Spray

If your beauty routine includes spraying your entire 'do to keep it in place, you probably have a film of hair spray on your bathroom vanity and walls. Easily remove it with a solution of two parts water and one part liquid fabric softener. Wipe on with a damp cloth, then rub off with a clean one.

Cut Down on Cleaning

You've just spent what seemed like an entire day cleaning your bathrooms. Now keep them that way by applying mineral oil all over shower doors and tiled surfaces. This will delay mineral build-up and cut down on future cleaning time.

Who Knew? Readers' Favorite

Stinky litter box? A great way to keep cat litter smelling fresh is to mix in a bit of baby powder each time you change the litter.

Drain Maintenance

Don't wait until your drain gets clogged before you flush out grime, grease, and hair. Perform monthly maintenance with the help of a little yeast. Pour two packets of dry yeast and a pinch of salt down the drain, then follow with very hot water. Wait a half an hour, then flush again with hot water. The yeast reproduces and expands, which breaks up stubborn grime and hair clogs and saves you from calling the plumber.

Down the Drain

If you have a clogged drain, try this before springing for expensive drain uncloggers that are harmful to your pipes. First, remove all standing water so you can access the drain. Then pour 1 cup baking soda down the drain, immediately followed by 1 cup table salt, and then ½ cup white vinegar. Let stand for 5 minutes, then pour 1 to 2 quarts boiling water down the drain. The baking soda, salt, and vinegar will dissolve any organic matter (like hair or grease), while the water will flush it out.

Get the Most from Your Plunger

Add a little petroleum jelly to the rim of your rubber plunger. It helps achieve great suction, so the disgusting job ahead is a little bit easier.

Bar Soap Solution

Always try to keep the soap in your soap dish dry. It will last much longer that way, and let's face it—picking up a soggy piece of soap to wash your hands is a bit on the disgusting side. Choose a soap dish that allows water to escape somewhere and your soap will stay solid!

Give Your Toothbrush a Bath

A great way to keep your toothbrush clean is to soak it overnight, every few weeks, in a solution of equal parts of water and baking soda. Rinse well before brushing again.

Bring Back Your Brushes

Revive hairbrushes and combs by soaking them in a pot of warm water and 1 tablespoon baking soda or ammonia.

Straighten Up Your Unruly Drawers

If your bathroom drawers are a jumbled mess, invest in an inexpensive plastic silverware tray. It's a great way to organize the little things you've got rattling around in there.

Frost a Window to Keep Out Prying Eyes

To create a temporary "frost" for a bathroom window, mix a solution of 1 cup beer and 4 tablespoons Epsom salts. Then paint the mixture onto the window. The paint will wash off easily.

Keep Cords Tidy

From blow-dryers to blenders to electric shavers, most small electrical appliances have cords that can get a little unwieldy. Keep them neat and out of the way with ponytail holders or rubber bands, or fold them up and store them in paper towel tubes—label the tubes to remind yourself which cord belongs to which appliance. This works well for storing Christmas tree lights, too.

Defogging Glass

What household item will cause mirrors or eyeglasses to stop fogging? Shaving cream! It's weird but true: Just rub glass with the cream, leave on for a couple of minutes, then rub off for a fog-free finish.

Bathroom Mirror Make-Over

Give your bathroom a little more ambience by running holiday lights around its perimeter. (For the best deals, wait until just after Christmas to buy the lights.) It works well as a night light, and you'll love the look when you're relaxing in the bath. To add even more decoration to a mirror, you can also repaint its frame or stencil a design around its edges.

CHAPTER 4

The Laundry Room

Are your clothes color-fast? Before using any stain remover, including the ones in this chapter, make sure to test it on an area of the garment that is inconspicuous. Allow the product to stand on the area for at least three to five minutes before rinsing it off. If there are any changes in the fabric's color, choose a different remover.

The Order of Things...in Your Washing Machine

Without order, we have chaos! Make sure to add the detergent at the proper point when doing your laundry. Your clothes will get cleaner if you turn the washer on while it's empty and add the detergent immediately. Let it dissolve and mix with the water before you add your dirty clothes. Putting detergent onto clothes that are still dry can cause dyes to fade and stains to crop up.

Cold for Clothes

No matter which temperature you choose to wash your clothes, always use a cold-water rinse. It will help the clothes retain their shape and color, and you'll save money and energy by not taxing your water heater.

Vinegar in Your Wash

If you suspect the rinse cycle isn't getting all the soap out of your clothes, add 1 cup white vinegar while they are rinsing. The vinegar will dissolve the alkalinity in detergents as well as give the clothes a pleasant fragrance.

All-Natural Fabric Softener

Fabrics made of from natural fibers do not need fabric softeners; only synthetics do. Add ¼ to ½ cup baking soda to the wash cycle to soften synthetic fabrics.

Sock Sorting the Easy Way

Use a mesh lingerie bag or pillowcase to launder each family member's socks separately. It's an easy way to keep them together, so they'll be easier to sort later.

Make White Socks White Again

Weird but true: Discolored socks will return to their original color if you boil them in a pot of water with a few slices of lemon.

Keep Jeans from Shrinking

Jeans are usually tight enough as it is! To minimize shrinking, wash them in cold water, dry them on medium heat for only 10 minutes, and then air dry them the rest of the way.

Keep Towels Looking Like New

Always add a cup of salt to the washing machine when laundering new towels. The salt will set the colors so the towels won't fade as quickly.

Add a big, dry towel to the clothes dryer when drying jeans and other bulky items. It will cut the drying time significantly.

Add Scented Salts for Beautiful Linens

Salt is a miracle worker when it comes to removing linen stains; and if you use scented salts in your laundry, you'll get the extra bonus of lovely-smelling sheets. Add ¼ cup scented bath salts during your washing machine's rinse cycle. Not only will your sheets smell great, but the salt acts like a starch to keep them extra crisp.

Don't Dry-Clean if You Don't Have To!

If a clothing label of a silk garment doesn't specify dry-cleaning only, you can wash it by hand. Silk should be hand-washed using cool water with mild liquid soap. Always air dry silk—never place it in the dryer, even on cool—and iron it from the "wrong" side of the fabric.

Wily with Wool

Dry-cleaning wool can cost some major money. Save money by using your washing machine instead. Wash wool with mild dishwashing liquid in cold water on the gentle cycle. If it's a blanket, air fluff to dry. If it's a garment, handle with great care, since wool fibers are very weak when wet. When getting rid of excess water, don't pull, stretch, or wring out the garment. Instead, roll it in a towel, squeeze the excess water out, and then dry flat.

Inside Out

Washing corduroy can be a nightmare, thanks to the amount of lint it attracts. To keep corduroy garments from retaining lint, wash them inside out. This also will keep acrylic sweaters from pilling.

Stain Quickie

Here's a great use for a clean-out plastic bottle (of the ketchup or salad dressing variety). Keep a mixture of water and laundry detergent, or your favorite stain remover, inside, and use it to quickly pre-treat stains on your clothing.

Fight with Fizz

If your clothes are extra greasy, add a can of lemon-lime soda to your washing machine along with detergent. The acid in the soda breaks down the oil in the greasy clothes, and your wash will sparkle.

Blame the Fabric Softener

Does it seem as though your clothes get greasy stains on them in the laundry? It may not be your imagination. One cause: Adding undiluted fabric softener. Remove these stains by pre-treating the fabric with a paste made of water and detergent, or use a commercial stain remover. Next time, dilute the fabric softener before you add it, or skip the stuff altogether and use vinegar instead.

Why the Sour Face for Lace?

If you own a lace tablecloth or doily that is beginning to turn yellow, let it soak in a bucket of sour milk for a few hours to return it to its former brilliant white. Just make sure to hand-wash it in mild detergent afterward!

Wrinkle-Free Curtains

Need to wash your sheer curtains but hate the thought of ironing them afterwards? Simply dissolve a packet of clear gelatin in the final rinse when laundering, and hang them up damp afterwards. The gelatin will remove almost all the wrinkles.

Who Knew? Readers' Favorite

Washing brightly colored fabrics for the first time often causes them to run, which can accidentally dye the rest of your wash! To keep your colors from running, wash them for the first time with salt. Add 1 teaspoon salt per gallon of water (about ¼ to ½ cup for a full load) to the washing machine the first time you wash a garment and its colors won't run.

Treat Ties Tenderly

Never try to remove a stain from a tie with water or you may create a large watermark that's hard to remove. Blot away excess stains (salad dressing, sauces, and gravy are popular ones) with a napkin or soft, white cloth. Take it to the dry cleaner as soon as possible; stains set after 24 to 48 hours. Don't attempt to rub the stain out or you could rub color from the fabric, especially if it's silk.

Who Knew?

Never mix stain removal materials, especially ammonia and chlorine bleach. The results could be dangerous!

The Best Stain Fighters

Buying expensive chemicals to treat stains on your clothing isn't necessary! Instead, use these all-natural remedies to remove drips and spills on fabric. To remove tough stains, you may have to apply a stain-remover more than once—if all else fails, just keep the garment near your washing machine and wash it over and over (applying the stain-remover each time) until the spot is gone. Just make sure the stain is gone before you dry the fabric in the dryer. The heat from your dryer can further set the stain.

- ✦ **Berries.** Soak the stain, overnight, in equal parts milk and white vinegar. Then launder as usual.

- ✦ **Blood.** Soak the stained area in club soda before laundering. If the blood is fresh (ouch!), make a paste of water and talcum powder, cornstarch, cornmeal, or meat tenderizer and apply it to the stain. Let it dry, and then brush it off.

- ✦ **Coffee.** To remove coffee stains, stretch the garment over a bowl, cover the stain with salt, and pour boiling water over the stain from a height of one to two feet. (The gravity helps.) Of course, always test first that the garment can withstand hot water (unlike, say, cashmere). Repeat a couple of times if necessary, but some of the stain (especially if it's not fresh) may remain. If so, treat with your usual spray-and-wash stain remover.

+ **Cosmetics.** Dampen stain with water and rub gently with a white bar soap (like Dove or Ivory), then rinse well and launder.

+ **Deodorants and antiperspirants.** Apply white vinegar, then rub and rinse. If the stain remains, repeat with rubbing alcohol, then launder.

+ **Dirt.** Rub shampoo over the area and let sit for 5 minutes before washing. For tougher stains, try pre-soaking in a mixture of one part warm water, one part ammonia, and one part laundry detergent.

+ **Gasoline.** Removing gasoline stains from clothing can be tricky. The most effective way we know of is to apply baby oil to the stain, then launder as usual. Since gasoline is an oil-based product, it takes another oil to pull out the stain and smell.

+ **Grass.** You can get rid of grass stains with toothpaste. Scrub it into the fabric with a toothbrush before washing. Or rub the stain with molasses and let stand overnight, then wash with regular dish soap by itself.

✦ **Grease.** Grease is one of the hardest stains to remove from your clothes, but if you catch it before it dries, you can remove it with baby powder. Apply baby powder to the stain, let it sit for an hour or so, and then wipe off the powder.

✦ **Gum.** Rub with ice until the gum hardens, then carefully remove it with a dull knife before laundering.

✦ **Ink stains.** Rub the area with a cut, raw onion, letting the onion juice soak in. Let sit for two to three hours before laundering.

✦ **Ketchup and tomato products.** Remove excess with a dull knife, then dab with a damp, warm sponge. Apply a bit of shaving cream to the stain, and let it dry before laundering as usual.

✦ **Mustard.** Hydrogen peroxide is effective at getting rid of mustard stains. After making sure the fabric is colorfast, apply a small amount to the stain and let set for several minutes before laundering.

✦ **Nail polish.** Unfortunately, the only thing that can remove nail polish is nail-polish remover. If the fabric can withstand this harsh chemical, work it in from the inside of the fabric by pressing it in gently with a paper towel.

✦ **Oil.** The best way to remove stains from cooking oil (olive, vegetable, canola, etc.) is with regular shampoo. Just make sure it doesn't have a built in conditioner.

✦ **Old or unknown stains.** If a stain is so old that it's set, try softening it up with vegetable glycerin. Glycerin can be found in health food stores, vitamin shops, and online. Apply some to the stain and let set for an hour before laundering.

✦ **Paint.** Treat the stain while it is still wet; latex, acrylic, and water-based paints cannot be removed once dried. While the paint is wet, rinse in warm water to flush the paint out, then launder. Oil-based paints can be removed with a solvent; your best bet will be to use one recommended on the paint can. If none is mentioned, blot with turpentine, rinse, and rub with bar soap, then launder.

✦ **Perspiration.** A great way to remove perspiration stains from white shirts is to crush 4 aspirin tablets into ½ cup warm water, and apply to the stain. Soak for at least three hours, and launder as usual.

✦ **Rust.** Remove rust stains by wetting the spots with lemon juice, then sprinkling with salt. Let the fabric stand in direct sunlight for 30 to 45 minutes.

✦ **Scorch marks.** Scorch marks will come out if you rub the area with a cut, raw onion and let the onion juice soak in thoroughly—for at least two to three hours—before washing. You can also try blotting the area with hydrogen peroxide.

✦ **Shoe polish.** Try applying a mixture of one part rubbing alcohol and two parts water for colored fabrics and only the straight alcohol for whites. Sponge on, then launder.

All Around the House and Garden

◆ **Tar.** Rub gently with kerosene until all the tar is dissolved, then wash as usual. Like with all stain removers, make sure to test a small area first to be sure the fabric is color fast. If you don't have kerosene, try petroleum jelly—just rub it in until the tar is gone. The jelly itself might stain the fabric, but it's much easier to remove with a spray-and-wash stain remover.

◆ **Tobacco.** Moisten the stain and rub with white bar soap (like Dove or Ivory), then rinse and launder.

◆ **Wine.** Blot the stain with a mixture of one part dishwashing liquid and two parts hydrogen peroxide. If this doesn't work, apply a paste made from water and cream of tartar and let sit.

How to Scrub Away Scuffs

If you have black scuffmarks on shoes, luggage, or other items, try rubbing lemon juice on them. Rubbing alcohol also works well.

Stuck Zipper?

Rub a beeswax-based candle or lip gloss on the zipper and the problem is solved! You can also try rubbing the zipper with the lead from a pencil.

As soon as you buy a pair of pants for your child, put some iron-on patches on the knees. Turn the pants inside out first, to ensure the patches won't show. Even though no one but you will know they're there, they will protect the vulnerable parts of your kids' pants, making them last much longer.

To Keep Your Thimble Nimble

Do you use a thimble to sew or sort papers? If so, wet your finger before you put the thimble on. This will create suction, so the thimble stays put.

Never Lose a Button Again

Dab a small amount of clear nail polish in the center of every button on a new garment. This seals the threads to the button, making lost buttons a thing of the past.

Iron Too Hot?

If you scorch a garment when ironing, cover the scorch mark with a vinegar-dampened cloth, then iron with a warm iron (not too hot). Presto! The burn is gone. For scorches on cotton garments, you can also use hydrogen peroxide or lemon juice instead. Just dab onto the scorch and leave out in the sun, which will bleach away the stain.

Cease Creases!

Creases in pants and other clothes can be hard to remove, especially if you accidentally ironed them in! To remove creases in fabric, use white vinegar. Just sponge a little on the crease with a damp sponge, then press with a warm iron.

Clean Your Iron (Not Your Pipes)

If only because they have the word "cleaner" in their name, we're always looking for ways to use pipe cleaners that don't involve crafts! Here's a good one: To clean the holes in your iron, dip a pipe cleaner in white vinegar and poke into each hole. Just make sure the iron is cool and unplugged!

Unclog Your Steam Iron

Another way to clean your iron is to pour equal amounts of vinegar and water into the water holder of the iron. Turn the dial to "steam" and leave it upright for five minutes. Unplug and let the iron cool down. Any loose particles should fall out when you empty the water.

Sticky Iron?

If your iron is beginning to stick to fabrics, sprinkle some salt on a piece of waxed paper and iron it. The salt will absorb the stickiness.

Iron Maintenance

To keep your iron smooth and clean on a regular basis, rub the bottom of it (while cold) with steel wool. Then heat it up and run it over an old, damp cloth. The steel wool will remove any debris, while the steam from the cloth will help clean it.

Dryer Sheet Freshener

After removing all your clothes from the dryer, save the dryer sheet! Place it at the bottom of trash bins to keep your garbage cans smelling fresher.

A Little Laundry Organization

Keep a small basket, or a bag on a hook, in your laundry area. It's a perfect place to throw all the miscellanea that you find in pockets or at the bottom of the washer—receipts, lip balm, pieces of paper, and tiny toys. Just don't throw any money in there—keep that for yourself!

Spring-Cleaning Prep

Get prepared for spring-cleaning by storing your cleaning products in a vinyl shoe holder, and hanging it on the back of your laundry room door. It's a great way to save space, and a reminder of the cleaning storm to come!

DIY Dehumidifier

You can make your own dehumidifier for the laundry room (or basement) without having to spend a lot in the process. Simply fill a coffee can with charcoal briquettes and punch a few holes in the lid. Place it in damp areas, and replace the charcoal once a month as it absorbs the humidity.

CHAPTER 5

Bedrooms

Citrus for Ceramic

The easiest way to clean ceramic figurines is to rub them with the cut side of a lemon wedge. Leave the lemon juice on for 15 minutes, then polish up with a soft, dry cloth.

The Answer for Artificial Flowers

To clean silk flowers, try blowing off the dust with a hairdryer set on cool. You can also put the flowers in a paper bag, add some uncooked rice, and shake. The dirt will transfer to the rice.

Who Knew? Readers' Favorite

Clean silk flowers easily by placing them, "bloom" end down, in a plastic bag with 2 tablespoons salt. Hold onto the stems and close the bag, then shake vigorously. The salt will attract the dust, leaving your flowers looking as good as the real thing!

Do-It-Yourself Headboard

To perk up your bedroom with a splash of color, get crafty with a DIY faux-headboard. Find a colorful sheet that complements the décor of your room; any fabric will work, so consider cotton, linen, velvet, and even fur! First, consider the width of your bed; a headboard should be slightly wider than your mattress. Then decide what style of headboard you like best, and cut your fabric to the right size and shape. Either wrap your fabric around a foam base and hang it on the wall, or hang it up on its own.

Bed Pillow Know-How

Here's an easy way to start your spring-cleaning: Begin with your bed pillows. To make them fluffy and fresh, just place them in the clothes dryer with fabric softener and two clean tennis balls for a few minutes.

Refresh Drapes and Bedspreads

The easiest way to freshen draperies and heavy bedspreads is to place them in your dryer with a damp towel, on the delicate cycle, for one half hour. For extra freshness, hang them outside afterward if the weather allows.

Quick Fix for a Saggy Mattress

To keep your mattress from sagging, it's a good idea to reverse it once a month. If it dips in the middle, place a few folded sheets under the center to even it out.

Radiator Energy Saver

Here's a great energy-saving tip for cold winter nights: If you have cast-iron radiators, tape aluminum foil to a sheet of cardboard (shiny side out) and place it behind the radiator. The radiant heat will bounce back into your room instead of being absorbed into the wall.

Close the Doors

In the summer months, make sure to keep your closet doors closed. Otherwise, you're paying to cool your closets, which will increase your energy bill.

Dusting a light bulb can increase the light in a room by up to 50 percent.

Reorganize for More Storage Space

Move your bed sheets and linens from the hallway linen closet to a top shelf in your bedroom closet. That way, they'll be closer to where they're actually used, and if you fold them properly, they won't take up much room. The major bonus? You've now freed up a valuable hallway closet to store something else.

Alleviate Dresser Drawer Mayhem

Is your dresser drawer starting to look like someone ransacked it? Egg cartons and plastic ice cube trays make great organizational tools for jewelry, cuff links, and other trinkets, and they'll easily fit inside your drawer.

The Pencil Is Mightier than the Sword?

Squeaky door hinges can be fixed with a pencil. Just rub the point over the hinge. Pencils contain graphite, which is an effective lubricant. Rubbing a pencil over the ridges of a stubborn house key will also help it slide into the lock more easily.

For Brass that Shines

Shining the brass hinges and knobs of your doors is easier than you think! Apply a white, non-gel toothpaste (a mild abrasive) to door fittings with a soft cloth, then rub. Use a fresh cloth to wipe clean, and your brass will sparkle! To protect brass between cleanings, apply a light coating of olive or lemon oil.

Extend Your Reach

If your spring-cleaning involves getting rid of cobwebs in hard-to-reach places, here's a hint: Untangle a wire hanger, and secure an old, clean sock to the end with a rubber band. Your arms just grew by three feet!

For Sweaty Summers

On sticky summer nights, cool down by sprinkling a little baby powder between your sheets before retiring for the night.

Smell the Roses Everyday

Clean laundry loses its fresh scent quickly when sitting in stuffy drawers and closets. To get your clothes, lingerie, and linens smelling freshly washed all the time, place fabric softener sheets in your dresser drawers.

Keep Drapes Fresh

Try this nifty trick to make sure your new or recently cleaned drapes stay crisp and fresh: Spray them with a few light coats of unscented hairspray before hanging them up.

Raise Matted Carpet

If a section of your carpet has been matted down by a piece of furniture, you can raise the nap back up with this simple ice cube trick. Let an ice cube melt into the matted area; wait until the next day to vacuum.

Just as Good as Sticky Tack

A terrific way to hang posters in your kid's room without leaving holes or stains is with white, non-gel toothpaste. Just put a generous drop on the back of each corner, press to the wall, and watch it stick.

Art Supply Storage

Keep art supplies in a clear, vinyl shoe bag hung from the back of your child's door. It's a smart, space-saving way to hold paints, pens, markers, brushes, and more.

Who Knew? Readers' Favorite

If the kids have drawn with crayons all of their bedroom walls, remove it with a bit of WD-40 spray, which works like a charm. Afterwards, you'll need something to remove the grease—we like a mixture of dishwashing detergent and white vinegar. If you don't have any WD-40, dip a damp rag into baking soda and rub on the mark to remove it.

The Ol' Chewing-Gum-Stuck-in-Hair Conundrum

Before you chop off a chunk of your kid's hair or attempt to shampoo it out, give this old trick for getting gum out of hair a shot. Massage a small amount of smooth peanut butter into the gum-stuck section of the hair. Yep, it really works: The oils in the peanut butter counteract the stickiness of the gum. If you're out of peanut butter, try mayonnaise or salad oil.

Time to Clean Teddy

To clean stuffed animals, just place them in a cloth bag or pillowcase, add baking soda or cornmeal, and shake. The dirt will transfer to the powder.

De-Grease Sticky Playing Cards

An oft-used deck of cards can get sticky and grimy from the oils on our hands. De-grease the cards by placing them in a plastic bag with a few blasts of baby powder. Give it a good shake before dealing the first hand.

Get the Bounce Back in Your Old Rubber Balls

Almost all soft rubber balls, including tennis balls, can be brought back to life by spending a night in the oven with only the pilot light on. The heat causes the air inside the ball to expand. Just be sure to remove the balls before you turn the oven on!

DIY Finger Paints for Little Da Vincis

Keep your kids busy and encourage their creativity with homemade finger paints: Start by mixing two cups cold water with ¼ cup cornstarch, then boil until the liquid is as thick as, um, finger paints. Pour into small containers, swirl in some food coloring, and watch your kitchen get trashed.

Dryer Lint Dough

Make a Play-Doh substitute for your kids with an unlikely ingredient: Dryer lint! First save up 3 cups of dryer lint, then stick it into a pot with 2 cups water, 1 cup flour, and ½ teaspoon vegetable or canola oil. Cook, stirring constantly, over low heat until the mixture is smooth. Then pour onto a sheet of wax paper to cool.

Homemade Bubbles!

Warm weather is bubble season for kids who want some outdoor fun. Here's an inexpensive homemade solution for blowing bubbles: Mix 1 tablespoon glycerin with 2 tablespoons powdered laundry detergent in 1 cup warm water. Any unpainted piece of metal wire can be turned into a bubble wand: Just shape one end of the wire into a circle. Blowing into the mixture with a straw will make smaller bubbles float into the air. For colored bubbles, add food coloring.

Freshen Up Stinky Diapers

If you get a nasty whiff every time you open the diaper pail, drop a few charcoal briquettes under the pail's liner. You'll be amazed at what you don't smell.

Never Buy a Baby Wipe Again

If you have a baby, you know that it's impossible to use fewer baby wipes. But you can save money by making them at home! Here's how: Combine 2 tablespoons each of baby oil and baby shampoo with 2 cups (cooled) boiled water and 1–2 drops of essential oil for scent (optional). Remove the cardboard roll from a package of paper towels, then cut the entire roll in half. Put some of the liquid mixture at the bottom of your container, then place the half-roll on top. Pour the rest of the liquid over your paper towels and voilà—homemade baby wipes! Let the wipes sit for about an hour to absorb all the liquid, and store in an old wipes container or a plastic bag.

CHAPTER 6

The Home Office

Lengthen Laptop Battery Power

If you clean the battery contacts on your laptop and cordless phone, the charge will last for a longer time. Use the tip of a cotton swab dipped in rubbing alcohol to clean the connection points.

Clean Up Your Keys

The easiest way to clean the gunk and dust between your computer keys is with transparent tape. Just slide a 2-inch strip between the rows of your keyboard, and the adhesive will pick up any debris.

Who Knew? Readers' Favorite

Unless it's cracked, skipping CDs are usually fixable. First, eliminate any dust and dirt by holding the CD under running water and rubbing with a soft, lint-free cloth to dry. To fix any scratches, rub a little white (non-gel) toothpaste into the scratch, then wipe with the damp cloth to remove any excess. The toothpaste won't repair the CD entirely, but it will at least keep it from skipping.

Label Madness

If you're like us, you receive free address labels in the mail from time to time. Put them to good use by labeling notebooks, kid's items, and anything else you'd like to personalize.

Lost Your Ruler?

If you need to measure something and don't have a ruler, grab a dollar bill instead. A dollar is exactly six and a quarter inches long.

Cuts Like New

Rehabilitate a pair of old scissors with these simple tips. First, remove any rust by applying a paste of salt and lemon juice, leaving for 15 minutes, and then rubbing thoroughly with a dry cloth. Then, sharpen the scissors by cutting a piece of steel wool or balled up aluminum foil 20 times or so.

Substitute Staple Remover

Need to remove a staple and don't have staple removers? Don't risk using your fingernail. Instead, use nail clippers. They work perfectly for removing stubborn staples.

Go-To Glue Remover

To remove glue residue on almost any surface, try vegetable oil on a rag. It's also an easy-breezy way to clean off residue from sticky labels. The vegetable oil neutralizes the glue's bonds.

Pen Accident?

A great way to remove ink from your skin is to mix some sugar with dishwashing liquid and rub into the spot. Unless, of course, the ink is a tattoo!

● Who Knew?

Use a thinner font to save when you print out documents. Thinner fonts like Times New Roman and Century Gothic will use up to 30 percent less ink than Arial.

Safely Store Important Papers

The school year is over, and you need a place to store the kids' artwork and diplomas. Try rolling them tightly in paper towel tubes so they won't crease, then label the outside, so you know what's what. The tubes can also be used to store marriage certificates and other important documents.

Protect Yourself from Identity Theft

Never carry your Social Security card in your wallet—if it's lost or stolen, thieves can use it to access all sorts of information about you. In addition, make a copy of the front and back of each credit card you carry, and store them in a safe place at home. That way, you'll be able to cancel those cards quickly if you need to.

Mail Safety Measure

Always put outgoing bills in a post office mailbox instead of the mailbox on your front door. A thief could get to your mail before the mailman, and the information provided in your letter could lead to identity theft.

Mail Management

If you're mailing out invitations, stick them in the mailbox on Wednesday, so that they'll arrive on Friday or Saturday. People respond more quickly to mail received on the weekend—so you'll get your headcount finalized sooner!

Postage Prescription

If you're sending a get-well card to a friend in the hospital, but aren't sure how long she'll be there, try this: Put the hospital's address on front of the envelope, and your friend's address as the return address.

That way, you're certain she'll get the card—at the hospital or once she returns home. (Just don't tell the post office!)

Unstick Stuck Stamps

If your postage stamps are stuck together, place them in the freezer for about 10 minutes. (Unfortunately, this doesn't work as well with self-adhesive stamps.)

Frozen Moments

If you discover a couple photos stuck together, don't lose hope! They can be unstuck. Place them in the freezer for half an hour, then gently break them apart with a butter knife. You can also slowly unstick them by blowing air on them from a hairdryer set on low.

Newspaper Mementos

To preserve special newspaper clippings, dissolve a Milk of Magnesia tablet in a shallow pan with a quart of club soda. Soak the paper for an hour, then let it lay flat to dry. Afterward, it's best to keep the paper under plastic in a photo album.

Eco-Friendly Gifting

Say "no" to Styrofoam popcorn! Instead, save your old egg cartons for the holiday season—they'll come in handy when packing up gifts to mail. Cut them up and use the pieces as packing material. It's cheap and environmentally friendly.

Finally, a Use for Old Telephone Cords!

If the cables in your office are a tangled mess of computer, printer, internet, and more, keep them tidy by running them through an old, coiled telephone cord. The coils will keep everything together neatly.

You can also use a few of the cardboard tubes from paper towels instead of a telephone cord.

Nonskid Drawers

A nonskid rug pad is a terrific liner for your office drawers. The tacky surface prevents paper clips, thumbtacks—anything!—from slipping around. It'll work well in your kitchen drawers too.

Unstick a Stuck Drawer

If your windows or desk drawers are stuck, simply rub a candle or white soap on the runners and the problem should be solved.

Who Knew?

To reduce the risk of neck and eye strain, make sure your computer monitor is 2–3 feet from your face, with the top of the monitor at (or just above) eye level.

Cleaning Your Computer Monitor

The most-asked home office question we get at our website, WhoKnewTips.com, is how to clean a computer monitor. Believe it or not, it's vinegar to the rescue again! Make sure your computer is off, then use a solution of one part vinegar to two parts water and apply it to the monitor with a soft cloth. To prevent streaks, make sure you move the cloth slowly in the same direction (top-to-bottom or side-to-side). Remove any remaining streaks with a chamois cloth.

CHAPTER 7

Your Car

For a Better Car Battery

The corrosion around your car battery posts can be cleaned easily with a thick solution of baking soda and water. Let it stand for 10–15 minutes before washing it off. Baking soda is a mild alkali and will neutralize the weak acid on the battery.

Tar on Your Car?

It's easy to remove tar from the outside of your car. Make a paste of baking soda and water, then apply it to the tar with a soft cloth. Let it dry, then rinse off with warm water.

Clean Car with Cornstarch

To clean dirty windows or your car's windshield, mix a tablespoon of cornstarch to about ½ gallon of warm water, and dry with a soft cloth. It's amazing how quickly the dirt is removed—and no streaking, either!

Club Soda Saver

One thing that never leaves our cluttered trunk (except when we're using it) is a spray bottle filled with club soda. Club soda does wonders for getting grime, bird droppings, and bug guts off your windshield. Just spray on, wait a few minutes, and turn on the wipers.

Smeary Windshield Wipers

Messy wipers are a safety hazard, and they're also pretty annoying. If your wipers are smearing the windows, wipe the blades with some rubbing alcohol.

Steel-wool pads make excellent whitewall tire cleaners. It's best to use the finest steel-wool pad you can find.

Make Car Cleaning Easier

One of the dirtiest parts of your car is usually its wheels, thanks to all the dark brake dust that accumulates there. Next time you clean your car's wheels, spray them with a light coat of vegetable oil when you're done. It will keep the dust from clinging, and you'll be able to wipe off the dust easily.

Bug Guts to Go

Don't you hate the smashed-up insects that seem to cover your car grille in the summer? The only thing worse than looking at them is trying to scrape them off, unless you try this trick: Spray a light coating of vegetable oil or non-stick cooking spray on your grille before screaming down the highway, and the revolting bugs will wipe off easily.

Zap the Sap!

Tree sap dripping on your car is one of the hazards of summer, but you can remove it easily with butter or margarine. Just rub the butter onto the sap with a soft cloth, and it comes right off.

De-Rust Your Bumper

The best way to remove rust from your car's chrome bumper? Just rub the rusted area with a shiny piece of crumpled aluminum foil that has been dipped in cola.

A Surefire Way to Wipe Away Window Decals

Transparent decals may be easily removed using a solution of lukewarm water and white vinegar. Place the solution on a sponge and dampen the area thoroughly for a few minutes. If this doesn't work, saturate the decal with straight vinegar and let stand for 15 minutes.

Who Knew? Readers' Favorite

Is it time to get rid of your "Gore 2000" bumper sticker? Try this: Set your blow-dryer on high and run it back and forth over the sticker until the adhesive softens. Then apply a bit of vegetable oil. Carefully lift a corner with a credit card, and peel it off.

Make Dashboard Scratches Disappear

Got scuffs and scratches on your odometer? You can eliminate the marks on dashboard plastic by rubbing it with a bit of baby oil.

Got a Stink in Your Car?

Instead of buying a commercial freshener, repurpose a sheet of fabric softener to sweeten the air. Place sheets under the car seats, in door pockets, or in the trunk to keep your car smelling fresh.

Is Your Car Winter-Ready?

Winterize your car battery so you don't get stuck in the cold. Pour a can of cola over the battery posts; let it sit for a half hour, then wipe it clean. Rub petroleum jelly on the posts before reattaching the battery cables. You should be good to go for the entire winter.

Forget the Ice Scraper

When the forecast calls for ice or snow, protect your car by placing two old bath towels across your windshield. When it's time to drive, simply pull off the towels and you're ready to go!

Ice Proof Your Windshield

If an ice storm is in the forecast, coat your windshield with a solution of one part water to three parts white vinegar. It will keep your windshield ice free.

Who Knew?

Never pour hot water on your windshield. The glass may expand from the heat and then contract as it cools, causing the windshield to crack.

Ice Ain't Nice

In the winter months, the only thing worse than having ice all over your windshield is having to spend a lot for a windshield deicer. Here's an inexpensive, yet effective, alternative to deice your windshield and windows: 1 part antifreeze, 4½ parts alcohol, and 4½ parts water.

Prevent Car Freeze Out This Winter

If your car doors freeze shut during the frigid winter months, try this preventative measure: Rub vegetable oil on the rubber moldings around your doors. Since it's the rubber, not the metal, in your doors that freezes, lubing it with oil should do the trick.

Prepare Your Car for Winter Weather

Before winter hits, fill a few old milk cartons with sand or kitty litter and keep them in your car's trunk. If you get stuck, sprinkle the sand on the ice to improve the tires' traction.

Stuck in the Mud?

If you get stuck in snow or mud, try using your car floor mat for traction. Better yet, be prepared and keep a blanket in the trunk for this very purpose.

Who Knew?

If you see any red spots on your driveway where you've parked your car, take it to a mechanic as soon as possible. The red liquid is mostly like your power steering fluid, and a bad leak can make it hard to handle your car, especially in an emergency.

Spend Less on Car Supplies

Specialty items used to clean cars are often found in big box and hardware stores. However, you'll find the same items—squeegees, shams, and sponges—for much less in the cleaning aisle of your local grocery store.

CHAPTER 8

Your Garden and Yard

Bid Adieu to Oil Stains

Cleaning oil spots off the driveway is difficult, and the cleaners can be quite expensive. Instead, sprinkle baking soda over the stains, then rub with a wet scrub brush with hot water. The baking soda breaks apart oil particles, so with a little elbow grease you can have your driveway sparkling in no time.

Get Rid of Grease

Another way to remove a grease stain from your concrete driveway is to rub kitty litter into the stain and let it stand for one to two hours before sweeping it up. The super-absorbent litter will soak up the stain.

Tidy Up the Driveway

You can keep paved areas looking spiffy with this trick. To remove unwanted grass or weeds from sidewalk and driveway cracks, squirt them with a solution of 1 gallon vinegar, 1 cup salt, and 8 drops liquid detergent.

Sidewalk Clean-Up

Want to get rid of the grass growing in the cracks of your sidewalk or patio? Make a mixture of salt and baking soda, sprinkle it on and sweep it into the cracks, and the problem should be solved.

Stains on Stones?

If you have stains on paving stones or a concrete patio, sometimes the solution is simple. Try pouring hot water from several feet above the stone onto the stain. Repeat several times, and your stain may just disappear. If this doesn't work, try rubbing some dishwashing liquid into the spot with a toothbrush, then rinsing off. For really tough stains, try adding a bit of ammonia to the water.

Never hang lights on a metal fence, even if the lights are approved for outdoor use. There is still a hazard of electric shock.

Algae Antidote

Your birdbath used to be a hot spot for the feathered folk, but ever since it became slimy with algae they've stayed away! Make your birdbath as fresh as new by emptying the water, then covering it with bleach-soaked paper towels or newspaper. After letting the paper sit for 5–10 minutes, remove it and rinse the bath thoroughly. Then fill it with fresh water and watch the birds enjoy. To attract even more birds to your birdbath, just cover the bottom with multi-colored marbles.

The Garden News

Old newspapers make terrific weed screens when planting your garden. Just spread the paper on the dirt, hose it down, and cover with mulch or more dirt. Plant your garden right on top and the newspaper will keep weeds from invading your flowers' space.

Grow Your Seeds in the Daily Rag

What's black and white and warm all over? If you're a seed, the answer is newspaper. Seeds need warmth, but not light, to germinate, so if you place newspaper (black and white only) over a newly sown area, it will keep the seeds warm and block out the light.

Fruity Seed Starters

Save orange and grapefruit halves for use in your garden. They make great containers for starting seeds. Just fill them with soil and seeds, and plant them. After the seeds germinate, the holders will decompose, leaving nutrients in the ground.

Eggshells are a great fertilizer for seedlings. Get a head start on your garden by first sowing them indoors in eggshell halves. Let them grow in an egg container, and when it's time to transplant them outdoors, just dig a hole for the shells.

Clear the Way for Lilacs

Lilacs hate grass. More specifically, they must compete with grass and any other vegetation for food and water. To help your lilacs flower beautifully, keep a 16- to 24-inch circle around the base free from grass. Lime and manure are great fertilizers for lilacs.

Give Pansies a Boost

If you've got pansies in your garden, take the time to pinch out the early buds. It encourages the flowers to grow, and you'll ultimately get more flowers this way.

Feed Your Fern

Banana skins and eggshells are excellent natural fertilizers, and the minerals they provide are not readily found in many synthetic fertilizers. Flat club soda is another great option for your garden: To perk up colors, give your plants an occasional sip or two.

Roses Look Better with a Little Fat On Them

Want to give your roses an extra dose of fuel? A small amount of fat drippings placed at the base of a rose bush will keep it healthier and make it bloom more frequently.

Get Your Wicker Ready for Spring

Make sure your wicker furniture is front-porch ready for the spring and summer months. Blow-dry off the loose dirt, then clean with white vinegar and warm salt water, and apply a coat of lemon oil.

Quick Clean for Your Patio Furniture

The easiest way to clean plastic or resin patio furniture? Just toss them in the swimming pool before going to bed, and in the morning they'll be good as new. Meanwhile, your pool's filter will clean up the dirt.

Who Knew? Readers' Favorite

The rain stopped just in time for your outdoor party, but not in enough time for the grass to dry before you want to mow it. To solve this problem, simply spray the blades of your lawnmower with vegetable oil, and the grass won't stick!

Let Your Lawn Grow to Starve Weeds

Try to keep your lawn about 3 inches high. The higher the grass, the less direct sunlight for pesky weeds.

Watch That Hose!

When watering your garden with a hose, take care not to drag the hose over your plants. Place a few short, heavy stakes in your garden to create an alleyway for the hose, restraining it from rolling around and distressing the delicate plants. If you don't have stakes, simply cut a wire hanger into six-inch pieces, bend them into arches, and use them to guide your hose.

Store Your Hose Properly for Maximum Usage

Your garden hose will last twice as long if you store it coiled, rather than folded. Try coiling it around a bucket. Note that the hose will be easiest to work with when it's not very cold or very hot outside.

Wooden Tools Need Love Too

Care for wooden garden tools as you would your skin and your plants—moisturize! Over time, wood dries out and splinters. Apply a thin coat of linseed oil to wooden handles on rakes and shovels; it'll keep them safe and usable. A little goes a long way, so use the oil sparingly.

Keep Your Trash Bag in Place

When you're raking leaves, nothing is more frustrating than a plastic trash bag that slips down into the garbage can. Rest easy, friends: All you need to do is secure the bag with a bungee cord (or two) and get to work. Fold the open end of the bag over the rim of the trashcan and wrap the cord around the outside to hold it in place.

Prune Plants Safely

Take care when pruning your roses and other thorny plants in the garden—you don't want to prick your fingers. Try holding the branches with a pair of kitchen tongs while you snip.

Tie Up Your Plants with Stuff You Don't Need

If you still have old, unused cassette tapes laying around, pull out the film and use it to tie up your plants. Better yet, old panty hose also makes an effective tie: Just cut the nylons into narrow strips. This works better than plastic ties because the panty hose expands as the plant grows.

Turn Old Nylons Into Plant Holders

Got an unwearable pair of nylons? Don't trash 'em yet! Nylon stockings or panty hose make excellent storage containers for plant bulbs. Air is able to circulate, which helps avoid mold. Store in a cool, dry location.

● Who Knew?

About 43 million Americans grow their own fruits and vegetables in a garden.

Safe Transport for Your Plants

When transplanting, always use lightly moistened soil and peat moss to help retain moisture in the roots. If the soil is dry, it won't hold together well during the transplant, which might result in a messy move at best and a plant casualty at worst.

Prevent Leaks When Re-potting Plants

If you are going to re-pot a plant, place a small coffee filter on the bottom of the new pot to keep the soil from leaking out the drainage holes. Not a coffee drinker? Try a paper towel or napkin instead.

For a Colorful, Sunny Garden

Be bold when planting flowers in sunny spots. Pastel-colored flowers can look washed out in bright sun, so consider bold reds and oranges for your flowers when planting in full sun.

Sappy Hands?

We don't like to be too sappy, especially on our hands! The easiest way to remove sticky tree sap from skin is with butter. Simply rub butter or margarine into the spots and wash with water.

Get Rid of Garden Stains

To remove dirt, grass, and other garden stains from your hands, add ½ teaspoon sugar to the soap lather before you wash your hands. You'll be amazed how easily the stains come off!

Remedy for Super-Dirty Hands

Kids playing in the mud? Powdered laundry detergent makes an excellent hand cleaner for very dirty hands. It's specially formulated to get rid of grease and oil, and the powder will work as a mild abrasive.

Disgustingly, door mats can capture more than a pound of dirt per square foot! Invest in good quality entrance mats, for both outside your door and inside.

Stow Your Wicker for the Winter

Before the first freeze arrives, bring all your wicker furniture inside to protect it from the cold. Freezing will cause the wicker to crack and split, which unfortunately is impossible to repair.

Frugal Furniture Covers

No space to bring outdoor furniture inside in bad weather? Instead of buying pricey furniture covers, protect lawn chairs and tables by covering them with large plastic bags.

Guard Outdoor Light Bulbs from Winter Wear

Before it gets too cold, consider applying a thin layer of petroleum jelly to the threads of all your outdoor light bulbs. It will prevent them from rusting and make them easier to replace when they blow out.

Shovel Snow Without Killing Your Back

Shoveling wet, heavy snow is a backbreaking job, but you can make it easier with a simple tip: Just coat your shovel with vegetable shortening or car wax, and the snow won't stick. If you're using a snowblower, coat the inside of the chute.

Don't Stand On Icy Ground—Melt It!

Make your winter season safer by salting icy ground in the most effective way possible. Use a lawn seeder or fertilizer spreader to distribute salt or sand in a thin, even layer. And don't forget to watch your step!

Getting Rid of Ice Naturally

To remove ice from your driveway or sidewalks without using harsh chemicals, mix 3 drops dishwashing liquid with 1 gallon boiling water and pour it onto the ice. The hot water will melt the ice, and the dishwashing liquid will prevent it from re-forming. Follow this up by sprinkling baking soda on the spot for extra traction.

Who Knew?

Commercially produced rock salt for de-icing surfaces doesn't work at temperatures lower than 5° F. Wait until it warms up a bit before you try to use salt to get rid of ice!

Sledding Solution

If a snow storm has just hit your area, you're going to have a hard time keeping your kids inside. If you don't have any sleds but they still want to be able to glide down hills, grab some garbage bags and tie the handles around their waists. They can sit on the bags and slide to their hearts' content.

Getting Rid of Pests

Killing Roaches the Green Way

Nothing is more revolting than roaches, except perhaps the chemicals we use to kill them. Try using this natural pesticide: Make a mixture of equal parts cornstarch and plaster of Paris, and sprinkle it in the cracks where roaches appear. If you're lucky, they'll be a thing of the past.

Say Bye to the Flies

The easiest way to get rid of fruit flies is to limit their access to their favorite foods. Let your fresh fruit ripen in closed paper bags. Then, after they ripen, store them in the refrigerator.

Fruit Fly Formula

To eliminate fruit flies naturally, fill a spray bottle with 10 parts water and 1 part rubbing alcohol, and spray away. It's about as effective as an insecticide, but not nearly as harmful to your family.

Herbal Help

A number of herbs will ward off crawling insects. The most potent are fresh or dried bay leaves, sage, and cloves. Place any of these herbs in locations where a problem exists, and the critters to do an about-face and leave the premises. Ants, roaches, and spiders may be more difficult to get rid of. If the these herbs don't work, try mixing 2 cups borax with an equal amount of sugar in a large container, and sprinkle the mixture in areas that you know the pests frequent. When crawling insects cross a fine powder, it removes the waterproof layer from their bodies, causing water loss and, ultimately, death.

Repel Flying Insects

It's not just for pesto! If you have a problem with any type of flying insect, keep a basil plant or two around the house. Drying the basil leaves and hanging them in small muslin bags will also repel flying insects—they hate the sweet aroma.

Clove's the Way

Silverfish are disgusting, down to each and every one of their legs. An effective, natural way to repel them is with whole cloves. Just sprinkle a few in drawers and other areas where you see them.

A Not-So-Happy Ending for Carpenter Ants

Get rid of carpenter ants naturally with this formula: Mix one packet dry yeast with ½ cup molasses and ½ cup sugar, and spread on a piece of cardboard. Leave this sticky trap wherever you see the ants, who will come in droves to the sweet smell. Unfortunately for them, they'll also get stuck. Wait until your molasses mixture is covered with the creepy pests, then throw away.

Mealworm Menace

Keep a few sticks of wrapped spearmint chewing gum near any open packages of pasta, and they'll never get infested with mealworms.

If you can figure out where ants are entering your house, you can keep them out. Simply sprinkle salt, cinnamon, chalk dust, or ashes on the their path of entry, and they'll turn around and go elsewhere.

A Mouse's Favorite Food

Though cartoons would have us believe otherwise, mice love the flavor of peanut butter even more than cheese. If you're having problems trapping a mouse with cheese, try smearing peanut butter on the trap instead.

A (Dead) Mouse House

If you're squeamish about having to pick up the remains of a rodent you've set a trap for, place the baited trap inside a brown paper lunch bag. Rodents like exploring small spaces, and once the trap has done its trick you can scoop it right up and throw it away.

Mice Hate Mint

If you're suffering from a mouse infestation and can see the mouse holes, smear a bit of mint toothpaste nearby and the smell will deter them. You can also rub toothpaste along the bottom of your baseboards and anywhere else mice may get into your home.

Peppermint for Pests

In addition to mice, moles, squirrels, gophers, and rats also hate the aroma of peppermint. Try planting mint near your home—chances are you will never see one of these pests again! For a preexisting gopher problem, soak cotton balls in peppermint oil and then drop them down gopher holes.

Keep Flies Away from Their Favorite Places

If you don't keep trash cans and compactors sealed tight, you can end up with a swarm of flies, pronto. Luckily, flies are repelled by lavender oil. Soak a few cotton balls with the oil and toss them into your garbage at the beginning of each week. The flies will stay away and your garbage won't smell as bad! Other natural repellents that will send flies in the other direction are oil of cloves and wintergreen mint sprigs.

Keep Plants Pest-Free

When watering outdoor plants, place a few drops of dishwashing liquid into the water, and make sure it gets on your plants' leaves. The detergent will keep bugs away, making sure your plants remain healthy and beautiful.

Solve a Snail or Slug Problem

Need to get rid of snails or slugs in your garden? Find the cheapest beer you can, then pour it into several shallow containers (shoeboxes lined with aluminum foil work well). Dig a few shallow holes in your garden and place the containers inside so that they are at ground level. Leave overnight and the next morning, you'll find dozens of dead (or drunk) snails and slugs instead. These critters are attracted to beer (who isn't!), but it has a diuretic effect on them, causing them to lose vital liquids and die.

Clear Out Slugs with Cabbage

If you're having problems with slugs eating your flowers and nothing seems to work, your solution might be in the form of distraction. Slugs love cabbage, so planting a few in your garden will ensure they stay away from your flowers and go for the cabbage instead.

Who Knew?

If you find a toad in your garden, tell it "thanks" and send it on its way. A single toad will feast on more than 100 slugs, cutworms, grubs, caterpillars, and assorted beetle larvae every night. If the toad is in top form, it can consume more than 10,000 invaders in just three months!

Save Your Plants

If you want to keep bugs off your plants, try spraying their leaves with a solution of 10 parts weak tea and one part ammonia. Try it first on a few leaves to test for damage, and make sure pets and children don't try to eat or lick the leaves (hey, they've done weirder things!).

For Crawling Critters

Sometimes, getting rid of insects is as easy as making it hard for them to get where they're going. Smear petroleum jelly around the base of plant stems, and ants and other crawling insects will slide right off, protecting your plants.

Buh-Bye, Bambi!

Hanging small pieces of a deodorant bar soap on trees will keep deer from munching on them. Or, try a piece of your clothing that you've worn for several days—deer don't like the smell of humans.

Rotten Eggs Are Good for Something!

Keeping deer, antelope, elk, and other large animals away from your garden and trees is a breeze with eggs that have gone bad. Just break them open (outside of the house) around the area that you want to keep the critters away from. The smell of hydrogen sulfide from the rotten eggs will keep them away long after you can no longer smell the offending odor.

Who Knew? Readers' Favorite

Spray your garbage cans with a mixture of one part ammonia and three parts water on a regular basis to keep squirrels, raccoons, dogs, and other critters from rummaging through the cans.

Foil Birds with Foil

If birds or other critters are nibbling at your fruit trees, trying hanging long strips of aluminum foil from the branches. They'll be attracted to its shiny surface, but once they bite it, they'll fly away.

Get Rid of Bothersome Bees

No one likes having to worry about a bee hijacking their soda while having a drink outside. So sip in confidence by covering the top of your drink with aluminum foil, then sticking a straw through the top.

Picnic Peace

To win the war against ants at your picnic, place the picnic table's legs in old coffee cans filled with water. The ants won't be able to climb up the table, and your food will stay safe.

Wasp Reduction

If you find a large wasp's nest, have it removed professionally. But for smaller numbers of these freaky fliers, fill a jar with half jam and half water. Cover with paper punctured with holes to attract, trap, and drown them.

Who Knew?

Unlike bees, wasps can sting again and again. If you spot wasps flying to one spot, look for a nest, which can produce up to 30,000 wasps! Contact your local health authority to remove it without delay.

Great Trick for Window Boxes

If you keep plants in window boxes, paint them white first. The bright, reflective surface will deter insects and reduce the risk of dry rot. It looks great, too!

Give Flies the Brush-Off

If you prefer not to use chemicals to get rid of flies, and you're not the most accurate fly swatter, invest in a strong fan. Scientists say that flies' wings are unable to operate in a breeze above 9 miles per hour, so open the windows, turn the fan to full power, and they'll soon buzz off. This is also a great trick for an outdoor party—just aim a few fans at the center of the action instead of spraying down your yard with awful-smelling repellant.

Free a Bee, Don't Smack It

If a bee or other stinging insect gets trapped in the car with you, do NOT swat at it! Instead, pull your car off to the side of the road, open all the windows or doors, and let the critter fly out.

Moth Trap

Trap moths by mixing one part molasses with two parts white vinegar and placing the mixture in a bright yellow container. The moths will be attracted to the color and the smell, then drown inside.

Keep Wool Safe

Placing your woolen clothes in a well-sealed bag isn't always enough to keep moths away, as any eggs laid in them beforehand will hatch—and the new moths will have a field day. To make sure all the eggs die before you put your clothes in storage, place the airtight bag of clothes in the freezer for 24 hours.

Who Knew? Readers' Favorite

When winter rolls around, do your sweaters smell like mothballs? Ick. Mothballs work great, but leave a nasty odor. When you're storing winter clothes next year, put a few leftover soap slivers in a vented plastic bag, and add it to your closet or cedar chest instead of mothballs. The soap will keep moths from damaging your clothes, and it smells fresh too.

Flea Flicker

Fleas can be eliminated from upholstery and carpets by vacuuming with a high-powered vacuum cleaner (ideally with a canister) with a bag that seals well. Remove the bag and dispose of it outside as soon as you finish.

Flea Fix

To get rid of fleas on your poor pet's skin, don't spring for expensive flea medication. Instead, add a garlic capsule to your pet's food each day. The smell secreted by your pet will not only deter fleas, but the garlic will help prevent roundworm.

A Good Night's Sleep for Your Pet

To ward off fleas from a pet's sleeping area, try sprinkling a few drops of lavender oil in the area. Fleas hate the smell of lavender oil, and will find somewhere else to hide. Your pet, meanwhile, can enjoy a good night's sleep—and smell great in the morning.

Spray to Lead Bugs Astray

If flies or bees have invaded your home or garden, squirt a little hairspray into the air. They hate the stuff and will go elsewhere.

Repel Bugs Naturally

Don't spend money on bug sprays. Their main ingredient is usually alcohol, so save some money by simply making a mixture of one part rubbing alcohol and four parts water, then spraying it on as you would bug spray. Another natural (and great-smelling) alternative is equal parts water and pure vanilla extract.

Studies have proven that electric bug zappers have no effect on mosquitoes. They seem to have a special sense that keeps them away from magnetic fields. If you're trying to keep mosquitoes away from your porch, citronella candles will work much better.

Catnip Repellant

For an effective personal insect repellent, rub fresh catnip leaves over exposed skin—just stay away from friendly cats!

Relief from Chigger Bites

Chigger bites? Aspirin helps—but not in the way you might think. Make a thick paste by crushing several aspirin tablets and then mixing in a bit of water. Rub the paste on any bites and it will ease the pain and itching.

Eliminate the Itch

Getting lots of mosquito bites can turn a fun evening into a harrowing one. Alleviate itching after the fact by applying a mixture of rubbing alcohol and hand soap to the bites. It will make them practically disappear.

Try a Little Tenderness...for Bug Bites

If you've just come back from a long weekend camping, you'll love this tip. Use meat tenderizer to treat insect bites! Moisten a teaspoon of tenderizer with a little water and rub it immediately into the skin. Commercial meat tenderizers contain papain, an enzyme from papaya.

Papain's protein-digestive properties will help decompose the insect venom.

Ease Insect Stings

Been stung by an insect? It's lavender oil to the rescue! Rub a bit directly onto the sting to alleviate the pain. Or, mix a paste of baking soda and water and apply.

Onions for Bee Stings

If you're stung by a bee, relief may be as close as the condiment plate at your picnic! Place slices of onion on a bee sting and the pain will start to lessen in about 15 minutes. Chemicals inside the onion break down the chemicals that make stings painful.

Another Treatment for Itchy Bites

Here's our favorite remedy for bug bites that won't stop itching: Add two Alka-Seltzer tablets to a small glass of water, then dip a Q-tip into the water and apply to bites. The aspirin in the Alka-Seltzer tablets will help ease the itch.

CHAPTER 10

Home Repair

Thaw Frozen Pipes Before They Burst

When temps drop to freezing, be on alert for frozen pipes in your walls, attic, or basement. Should a pipe burst, you might be left with some serious and costly damage. If your pipes are frozen but haven't yet burst, find the suspected area (often in an exterior wall), turn on your faucets, and use a blow-dryer to thaw it out. As always, though, take care that the appliance doesn't get wet.

Moving Marble

If you're moving a large piece of marble, such as a tabletop, always transport it upright. If you carry it flat, it can crack under its own weight.

Repurpose Wine Corks

Slice old corks into thin disks, then glue them to the feet of your heavy furniture. It's a great way to protect your floors, and makes moving the furniture a bit easier.

Walls Have Cavities, Too!

Small holes in your white wall? It's toothpaste to the rescue! Simply dab a small amount of white (non-gel) toothpaste into the hole and you'll never notice again—or, at least, your guests won't!

Protect Your Walls from Cracks

Before driving a nail into a plaster wall, place a small piece of tape over the spot you're working on. This simple prep step will prevent cracking in the plaster.

According to home improvement store Lowe's, almost 75 percent of their customers are women.

Got Grease Stains on Your Wall?

If grease is still visible on the wall after removing wallpaper, apply a coat of clear varnish to the spots. The grease won't soak through to the new wallpaper.

Wallpaper 101

Hanging wallpaper? Try using a paint roller instead of a sponge to apply paste before you hang it, and then to smooth it out afterward. You'll get more coverage per stroke.

Make Your Own Swatch Book

When painting in your house, it's always a good idea to keep track of paint colors—you may need them to match future paint jobs or to help you coordinate other items in the house. Create swatches by dipping a 3-by-5-inch index card into your paint can and writing down the details.

Speed Up a Paint Job

Quicken your interior paint jobs by mixing a quart of semigloss latex paint into a gallon of flat latex paint. The finish won't shine more than it would with straight flat paint, but the paint will glide on and cover much more easily.

Don't Let Your White Paint Yellow

Some white paints can yellow in a matter of months, making the paint job look much older and staler than it really is. Keep your white walls white by adding 7–10 drops of black paint to each quart. Also, when selecting your paint colors, note that white paint will age better if exposed to natural light.

Remove a Painting Mistake

You've just painted your window trim, and got a big glob of "country yellow" on the glass pane. But there's no need to use a dangerous razor blade to remove the paint that spilled on the glass. Instead, remove the paint safely and easily with a pencil eraser. If the paint has dried, or is old, dab on some nail polish remover, wait a minute, then erase.

Who Knew? Readers' Favorite

Painting doors? Avoid getting paint on the hinges by coating them lightly with petroleum jelly before you start.

No Cleaning Necessary (for Now)

If you want to avoid cleaning a paint roller, wrap it in foil or a plastic bag and place it in the refrigerator. This will keep the roller moist and usable for a few days, so you can finish where you left off later.

The Art of Paintbrush Maintenance

Old, crusty paintbrushes put a cramp in our paint projects. To soften those bristles, we soak them in full-strength white vinegar and then clean them with a comb. To prevent brushes from hardening in the first place, after using and cleaning, rub a few drops of vegetable oil into the bristles to keep them soft.

Keep Your Paint Fresh for Longer

If you've got leftover paint, you can prevent it from drying up with this crafty maneuver: Blow up a balloon until it's about the size of the remaining space in the can. Then put it inside the can and close the lid. This will reduce the amount of air in the can, thus prolonging the paint's freshness.

Who Knew? Readers' Favorite

First, place a piece of plastic wrap under the paint can's lid, then make certain the lid is on tight before you turn the can over. The paint is exposed to less oxygen this way and will last much, much longer.

Avoid That Icky Paint Skin

If you've ever stored a partially used paint can, you've probably noticed that a skin of dried-up paint forms at the top of the can. To prevent this, place a piece of waxed paper the size of the opening on top of the paint.

Strain Out Lumpy Paint

If you have lumps in your paint, cut a piece of window screen just slightly smaller than the circumference of the can. Place it inside the can and let it settle to the bottom. It'll carry the lumps with it.

Guard Your Work (and Your Shirt) from

Dripping Paint

To catch drips while you paint, try this makeshift drip cup: Cut a tennis ball in half and slice a thin slot in the bottom bowl of one half. Then slide your brush handle through the slot so the bristles stick out of the open side. A small paper plate or cup works too.

Prevent a Dripping Paint Can

You know that little groove along the rim of a paint can that tends to fill up and spill paint all over the place? Using a nail or an awl, notch a few holes in there to create a drain for the paint, so it drips back into the can instead of dripping down the outside. Alternatively, you can place masking tape on the rim of the paint can before pouring—remove the tape later and the rim will be clean.

Who Knew?

If you are hiring someone to paint your house, you should be wary of anyone asking for more than 30 percent of the cost up-front. The standard is 10 percent.

Paint Roller Pan Liner

There's no need to spend your money on disposable paint liners for your roller pan. It's just as easy to line the pan with aluminum foil—and a lot cheaper too.

Quick Clean for a Paintbrush

The fastest way to clean a paintbrush? Put ½ cup liquid fabric softener in a gallon of water and vigorously swirl the brush in it for 20 seconds.

For Paint-Covered Hands

It's hard not to get paint all over yourself when painting a room. An old household trick is to wipe turpentine on your hands to get the paint off, but there's a much less smelly way! Simply rub your hands with olive oil, let sit a couple of seconds, then rub off with a damp, soapy sponge. Not only will the olive oil remove the paint, but it's great for your skin, too! For enamel or oil paint, rub your hands with floor paste wax, and then wash with soap and water.

Sticky Fingers (and How to Unstick Them)

If you glue your fingers together when working with a quick-bonding glue or epoxy, nail polish remover will do the trick. If you get stuck working with rubber cement, try lacquer thinner; you may need to let the thinner soak in for a few minutes before gently pulling your fingers apart.

Tip for the Butterfingers

How many times have you hit your fingers while hammering in a nail? Next time you're hanging pictures, put the nail between the tines of a fork before hammering. Your fingers will thank you, and your kids won't have to hear you swear.

Looking for a Stud? (In a Wall, That Is)

If you'd like to hang a heavy mirror or piece of art, you'll first have to locate a wall stud. Don't own a stud finder? No worries. Studs are normally 16 inches apart, so measure 17 inches from a corner to find your first stud. Keep measuring out by 16 inches until you find the stud nearest your desired spot. Alternatively, you can use a compass. Hold a compass level with the floor and at a right angle to the wall, and then slowly move the compass along the surface of the wall. When the needle moves, that's where you will find a stud.

When's Your Wood Smooth Enough to Use?

If you're sanding wood and want to know when it's smooth enough, use the panty hose test: Slip an old nylon stocking over your hand and run it over the wood. You'll have no trouble finding the slightest rough spot. Just don't wear those nylons afterwards!

Aged Wood Absorbs Stains Best

If you allow wood to "weather" before you apply a stain, the stain will last years longer. It's a case where patience pays off.

For a Smooth Varnish

Stir varnish thoroughly from the bottom of the can, but *don't* stir vigorously. Stirring can create air bubbles, which can ruin a smooth finish. If you notice air bubbles, brush them out while the varnish is still wet. If it's already dry, gently buff them out with very fine steel wool.

Flour Power

If you're painting old woodwork and need to patch small holes, fill them with flour and then paint. It will harden and not be noticeable.

Who Knew? Readers' Favorite

If you need to repair a hole in a piece of wood, add a small amount of instant coffee to the Spackle, or to a thick paste made from a laundry starch and warm water. The coffee tints the paste to camouflage the patched-up spot.

Window Screen Fix-Up

To repair small holes in window screens, cover them with a few of layers of clear nail polish. It will keep the hole from becoming bigger and prevent insects from coming through.

Tighten Droopy Cane Chairs

A chair's caning can loosen and begin to droop. If you let it go long enough, you might even fall through the seat and hurt your bum (not to mention your ego). But, no fear! You can tighten it easily and cheaply. Apply very hot water to the underside, then dry the chair in direct sunlight.

A Safe Ladder, with a Coffee to Go

Save up your used coffee cans for your next home-maintenance project. If you need to use a ladder on soft earth, set the legs inside those empty cans so they won't sink from your weight.

Saw Safety

Whether you keep saws in the workshop, tool shed, or basement, make sure to protect yourself and others from those dangerous blades. Use a split piece of old garden hose to cover them whenever they're not in use.

Nip Rust in the Bud

Prevent your tools from rusting now and avoid the annoying rust-removal process later. Place a few mothballs, a piece of chalk, or a piece of charcoal in your toolbox—all three eliminate moisture and fight rusting before it begins. If you've got nuts and bolts that are rusted together, just submerge them in cola for a day and they'll come apart easily.

Loosen a Rusty Nut or Bolt

To remove that pesky rusted nut or bolt, put a few drops of ammonia or hydrogen peroxide on it, and wait 30 minutes. If you're out of both, try a little bit of cola instead.

Squeak Tweak

Squeaky door and cabinet hinges, as well as sticky locks, benefit from a light spritz of a nonstick cooking spray. And it's cheaper than WD-40, too!

Safely Remove a Busted Light Bulb

To remove a broken light bulb from the socket, first turn off the electricity or unplug the lamp, and then push half of a raw potato or small apple into the broken bulb's base. Turn it to unscrew the base. Just don't eat it afterward!

Another Light Bulb Fix

Here's another easy, safe way to remove a broken bulb from the socket. After turning off the power, wedge a piece of bar soap into what's left of the bulb. Then twist and safely remove the broken bulb.

When using an electric drill or other power tool, try to plug it directly into the wall if you can. Using a long extension cord can cut down on the amount of electricity getting to the tool, making it turn more slowly.

Removing Resistant Nails

If you're trying to remove a nail from a wall that's lost its head, you can still take it out using the claw-end of your hammer. Simply grab the nail with the hammer, then move it from side to side over and over until you get the nail out.

For a Tight Screw

If you're having trouble removing a tough screw, try blowing hot air on it with a hair dryer for about a minute. The heat will expand the head of the screw, making it easier to remove.

Keep Wood from Splitting

If you're hammering a nail into a piece of wood and want to make sure the wood doesn't split, remove the sharp point of the end of the nail with a pair of strong wire cutters before grabbing your hammer.

PART TWO

Chef's
Secrets

Whether you're preparing a huge meal for a holiday or are just whipping up a snack for the kids, cooking conundrums are some of the most annoying. Whip your pancakes just a bit too much, and they'll be flat; add the barbecue sauce too soon and your ribs will burn—it's simple mistakes like these that can turn cooking into a chore. But in this section, we'll not only give you the how-to for making a hundred of your most-prepared dishes, we'll give you tips and tricks to make the little things (and few of the big) quicker and easier. Learn how to make your food last longer, and how to make every mealtime a success.

CHAPTER 11

Cooking Basics

Prepare for the Unexpected While Cooking

Professional cooks keep small plastic bags nearby in case both hands are covered with dough or food and they need to answer the telephone. Or, you could put your hands in plastic bags *before* mixing meatloaf or kneading dough.

Conserve Cooking Utensils by Planning Ahead

To use the fewest cooking utensils possible, first measure out all the dry ingredients, then the wet ingredients. This way, you can reuse the measuring spoons or cups without having to rewash and dry them.

Who Knew? Readers' Favorite

Before using a measuring cup to measure a sticky liquid like honey, coat the inside with vegetable oil or nonstick cooking spray. The liquid will pour out easily.

Improvised Spoon Rest

Who needs a spoon rest when you're at the stove cooking? Just rest your spoon on a piece of bread, which will catch all the juices and bits of food. Toss the bread when you're done cooking.

Dental Floss in Your Kitchen

A must-have for your kitchen toolkit is dental floss! (No, really.) Not only is it useful for trussing a turkey, but it's also great for bakers. Dental floss is perfect for cutting a cake without too many crumbs, and if your freshly baked cookies are stuck to the baking tray, simply hold a length of dental floss taut and slip it underneath the cookie. It works better than a spatula!

Knife Know-How

You've finally saved up enough to buy a brand new knife set (or, better yet, are compiling a gift registry). So which knives should you get? The three basic knives everyone should own are a chef's knife, for chopping and slicing; a paring knife for deseeding and other small jobs; and a boning knife, for cutting meat and poultry. Additional knives you may want to have are a serrated knife for slicing bread, a cleaver, a fish-filleting knife, and a pair of kitchen scissors.

● Who Knew?

A sharp knife is actually safer than a dull one. Dull knives are more likely to slip off foods, resulting in cut fingers.

Cutting Board Cues

Studies continue regarding the safety of plastic cutting boards versus wood ones. Most cooks have their favorite, and many use both. No matter what kind of cutting board you prefer, here are some safety and cleaning tips for them.

✦ Reserve one cutting board only for raw meats, poultry, and fish; use other cutting boards for prepping vegetables, cheeses, and cooked meats.

✦ Wash all cutting boards immediately after use in very hot, soapy water. If you have a plastic cutting board, run it through the dishwasher, which reaches higher temperatures than your sink does. To make sure you get every last bacterium, you can also wash the boards in a weak bleach solution.

✦ Remember that it's harder to scrub bacteria out of nooks and crannies; discard cutting boards whose surfaces have deep knife marks.

✦ Avoid setting hot pans on wood cutting boards or butcher-block countertops. Bacteria love heat, and the hot pan may serve to activate them or draw them to the surface of the wood.

✦ To quickly disinfect a plastic cutting board, wash it thoroughly, rub half a cut lemon over it, and microwave it for a minute.

✦ Another way to make sure you're getting the germs out of a wooden cutting board is to cover it with a light layer of salt to draw out any moisture from the crevices. Leave the salt on overnight before scraping it off. Then treat the wood with a very light coating of mineral oil. Make sure it is only a light coat, because mineral oil may affect the potency of a number of vitamins in fruits and vegetables.

✦ Do you have a cutting board that has a lingering odor that just won't quit? Remove the smell by rubbing the board with very salty water or some white vinegar.

Fridge Hygiene

Store cooked foods above uncooked meat in your fridge. This minimizes the risk of food poisoning caused by drips from uncooked meat and other foods. Wrap any food with strong odors and avoid storing them close to dairy foods, which can become easily tainted. And throw away that slimy lettuce at the back of the vegetable drawer!

Freezer Facts

You can freeze any food except canned or preserved food and whole eggs. Some foods, however, do not freeze well. High-fat dairy products like cream and mayonnaise tend to separate when defrosted, and high-water content vegetables such as lettuce and cucumbers will go soggy. Freezer temperature is critical for maintaining quality of foods. Keep your freezer set at 0° F.

Frosting Fix

Next time you defrost your freezer, spray it with a thin layer of cooking oil afterwards. The oil repels water (and ice), which will prevent it from frosting over. If it does frost over, you should be able to easily chip away the ice without having to defrost the entire freezer.

Ice Rinsing Remedy

When ice cubes stay in the freezer tray more than a few days, they tend to pick up odors from foods you have stocked away. Give ice cubes a quick rinse before using them to avoid altering the flavor of your beverage.

Who Knew?

The longer a food is frozen, the more nutrients it will lose. Seal all foods to be frozen as tightly as possible to avoid freezer burn and the formation of ice crystals. Ice crystals cause thawed food to become mushy.

Cook It Through

Contrary to popular belief, freezing doesn't actually kill bacteria or other food microbes, but what it does do is put them in a dormant state so they won't be active or reproducing until the food is thawed again. This is why it's important to cook food thoroughly after defrosting. If you defrost raw meat and then cook it thoroughly, you can freeze it again, but remember you should never reheat foods more than once. If you want to use a meaty sauce like Bolognese for several meals, reheat individual portions when you need them rather than the whole pot.

Slow Cooker Safety

Many people question whether a Crock Pot is safe for cooking foods, or if it's a breeding ground for bacteria because of its low temperatures. Most slow cookers have settings that range from 170–280° F, and most bacteria die at 140°, so you should be safe. However, to minimize the risk of food poisoning, follow these tips.

- ✦ Don't attempt to cook frozen or partially thawed foods, and don't use the cooker to reheat leftovers. (Uncooked foods at refrigerator temperature are safe to use.)

- ✦ Cook only cut-up pieces of meat—not whole roasts or poultry—to allow the heat to penetrate fully.

- ✦ Make sure that the cooker is at least half to two-thirds full or the food may not absorb enough heat to kill any bacteria.

- ✦ Cover the food with enough liquid to generate sufficient steam.

- ✦ Always use the original lid, and be sure it fits tightly. Never use the cooker with the lid off.

- ✦ When possible, cook on the highest setting for the first hour, then reduce it to low if necessary.

Avoid using a slow-cooker to cook vegetables. During prolonged cooking, most of the nutrients will be lost because of the heat.

Deodorize the Disposal

A quick and easy way to deodorize your in-sink garbage disposal is to grind an orange or lemon peel inside it every so often. It will get rid of grease and smell wonderful!

Vanquish Smells with Vinegar

To help control unpleasant cooking aromas, dampen a cloth with a mixture of equal parts vinegar and water. Drape it over the cooking pot, taking care that the edges are far from the flame or intense heat.

Remove strong food smells from your hands by rubbing them under cold running water while holding a stainless steel spoon in the same way as soap. Rinse with soap and water. Or try this old trick, reportedly used by people who made perfumes: Dunk your hands in coffee grounds, then wash with soap and water.

Easy Oven Cleaning

Save a lot of time in clean-up by lining the bottom rack of your oven with aluminum foil when cooking something messy. But be aware—you should never line the bottom of your oven with foil, as it could cause a fire.

Check the Temperature without a Thermometer

If you suspect your oven's temperature isn't in line with what it reads on the dial, but don't have an oven thermometer to test it, use this simple trick. Put a tablespoon of flour on a baking sheet and place it in a preheated oven for five minutes. If the flour turns light tan, the temperature is 250–325°. If the flour turns golden brown, the oven is 325–400°. If it turns dark brown, the oven is 400–450°. And an almost a black color means the oven is 450–525°. Figure out the disparity between what the temperature is and what it reads, and make sure to set your oven accordingly in the future.

Foil Foible

Never wrap foods that contain natural acids—like tomatoes, lemons, or onions—in aluminum foil. The combination of the foil and the acid in the foods produce a chemical reaction, which affects the taste of the food.

Protect Silver from Acidic Foods

Some foods are particularly harsh on silver: Olives, salad dressings, vinegar, eggs, and salt will all cause silver to tarnish quickly. Wash your silver as soon as possible after it's had contact with any of these items.

Cooking with Wine

When cooking with wine, try not to use too much, or the taste may well overpower the dish. Wine should only be used to improve the flavor. If you want to assure that you taste the wine in a recipe, just add it to the recipe about five to seven minutes before completion. And don't forget a little sip for the cook!

Who Knew?

The boiling point of alcohol is 173° F, much lower than the boiling point for water (212°). When alcohol is added to a recipe, it will lower the boiling point until it evaporates.

Avoid a Boiling Blunder

To keep a pot from boiling over, stick a toothpick between the lid and the pot. Other tricks include placing a wooden spoon across the top of the uncovered pot or rubbing butter around the inside lip of the pot.

Canola Cure

To sauté or fry with butter, margarine, or lard, add a small amount of canola oil to raise the smoke point. This will keep the solid fat from breaking down at lower temperatures.

Heat the Pan

When sautéing or frying, always heat your pan for a couple of minutes before adding butter or oil to ensure that nothing sticks and is heated evenly. It's also a good idea to sprinkle a little salt in your pan before frying—it will keep the oil from splattering.

Important Tips for Deep-Frying

Sometimes food sticks together when you're deep-frying it. To prevent this, lift the basket out of the oil several times before leaving it in for good. And don't try to fry too much at once—the oil may bubble over from the temperature difference of the cold food and the hot oil. And speaking of hot oil, be sure it's 300–375° F before you add the food.

● Who Knew?

Salt draws moisture from foods. If a food is salted before it goes into the fryer, the salt will draw moisture to the surface and cause the food to spatter when it's placed into the heated oil.

A Lighter Coat for Fried Foods

When making a batter for foods for deep-frying, try adding ½ teaspoon baking powder for every ½ cup flour. The coating will be lighter.

Frying Temperatures Are Critical

Oil needs to be at the proper temperature whether you're sautéing or deep-frying. If the temperature is too low, the food will absorb too much oil and become greasy, not crispy. If the oil is too hot, the food may burn on the outside and not cook through. Most breaded foods are normally fried at 375° F, but check the recipe. Chicken should be fried at 365° F for 15–20 minutes for white meat and 20–25 minutes for dark.

When Cooking with Oil

In terms of fat content, less oil is always better than more oil! So if you have to coat food with oil before sautéing or baking it, use a spray bottle rather than a brush to reduce the amount of fat that ends up on your food.

Unsalted Butter Is Best

If you sauté with butter, be sure you use the unsalted kind. When salted butter melts, the salt can separate from the butter and may consequently impart a bitter taste to the dish.

Tips for Breading

Keeping breading on foods can be a challenge, but there are a few tricks to try (other than using superglue). First, make sure that the food that is to be breaded is very dry. Use eggs at room temperature, and beat them lightly. If you have time, refrigerate the breaded food for an hour, then let it sit at room temperature for 20 minutes before cooking. Homemade breadcrumbs are better than store-bought because of their uneven texture.

Seasoning Saver

When changing the yield of a recipe, don't increase the seasonings proportionately or the recipe will taste wrong. If you're doubling the recipe, increase the seasonings only by one and a half; if you are tripling the recipe, double the amount of seasoning.

● Who Knew?

Drying intensifies the flavor of herbs, so fresh herbs are milder than dried.

Crushing Spices

Don't have a motor and pestle? A great way to mix and crush spices is to place them in a pan and press with the bottom of a smaller pan. A coffee grinder works well, too.

Herbal Flavor Booster

Crushing dried herbs before using them will boost their flavor, as will soaking them for a few seconds in hot water. This also works well if they have lost their flavor.

Great Garlic Tips

Garlic is one of our favorite seasonings, and we find it's much better fresh than in powdered form. If you love garlic too, here are some tips for cooking with this delicious ingredient.

✦ To make garlic easy to peel, soak it in very hot water for 2–3 minutes, or rinse it under hot water. This should loosen its skin.

✦ If your head of garlic sprouts, some of the flavor will go into the sprouts; however, the sprouts can then be used for salads.

✦ If you have added too much garlic to your soup or stew, add a small quantity of parsley and simmer for about 10 minutes.

✦ Mincing garlic is usually a sticky mess, but won't be anymore if you sprinkle the garlic with a few drops of olive oil beforehand. The oil will prevent the garlic from sticking from your hands or the knife.

● Who Knew?

Fragrance is the best indicator of potency in dried herbs: The greater the smell, the better the seasoning. If you're not hit with a wonderful fragrance when opening a jar of dried herbs, throw it out.

Pressing Ginger

If you're preparing a recipe that calls for crushed ginger, don't both with the side of the your knife. Simply peel the ginger and put it through a garlic press.

Save Some Zest for Later

Don't discard the rinds of limes, lemons, oranges, or other citrus. Grate them, then store in tightly covered glass jars in the fridge. They make excellent flavoring for cakes, and can be sprinkled over chicken and fish as well.

Make Seasoning Easy

Keep a shaker filled with a ratio of 75 percent salt and 25 percent pepper (or whatever ratio you usually use) next to the stove or your food-preparation area, and it will be even easier to season foods.

Who Knew?

Part of the appeal of herbs is the wonderful smell they impart to your dish. Add some or all of the herbs in your dish just before it is served, because the aroma (and some of the flavor) can dissipate during the cooking process.

The Baking Powder Test

Did you know that baking powder loses potency over time? If you can't remember when you bought it, you should test it before using it. Here's how: Put ½ teaspoon baking powder in a small bowl, then pour in ¼ cup of hot tap water. The more vigorously it bubbles, the fresher the baking powder. Try this test on a fresh box of baking powder so you will be familiar with the activity level of the fresh powder. Be sure to check the expiration date on the box when you first purchase it to be sure it's fresh. Once opened, baking powder will remain fresh for about a year.

The Baking Soda Test

If you are not sure how old your baking soda is, test its activity level. Stir ¼ teaspoon baking soda into about 2 teaspoons of white vinegar; it should bubble vigorously. If it doesn't, throw it out.

Why can't you simply substitute buttermilk for milk measure for measure in recipes? Chemically, the two are quite different. Buttermilk is much more acidic than regular milk and will interfere with any leavening agents, reducing the amount of carbon dioxide.

Cooking Substitutions

Preparing a recipe and realize you forgot one essential ingredient? Use the chart below to find a proper substitution. Unless otherwise noted, use the substitution in equal measure to the ingredient called for in the recipe.

Ingredient Called for	Substitute
Active dry yeast (one ¼-ounce envelope)	1 cake compressed yeast
Allspice	1 part ground cinnamon + 2 parts ground cloves or ground nutmeg (for baking only)
Anise seed	fennel seed
Apples (1 cup chopped)	1 cup firm chopped pears + 1 tablespoon lemon juice.
Arrowroot	use 2 tablespoons flour for every 4 teaspoons arrowroot

Ingredient Called for	Substitute
Baking powder (1 teaspoon, double-acting)	⅝ teaspoon cream of tartar + ¼ teaspoon baking soda or ¼ teaspoon baking soda + ¼ cup sour milk or buttermilk (lessen other liquid in recipe)
Basil (dried)	tarragon or summer savory or thyme or oregano
Bay leaf	thyme
Black pepper	cayenne pepper (use much less; start with a pinch)
Brandy	cognac or rum
Bulgur	cracked wheat or kasha or brown rice or couscous or quinoa
Butter	hard margarine or shortening; or oil if it is not a baked good
Buttermilk (1 cup)	1 cup milk + 1¾ tablespoons cream of tartar or 1 tablespoon lemon juice + milk to make 1 cup (let stand 5 minutes) or sour cream
Cake flour (1 cup)	1 cup minus 2 tablespoons unsifted all-purpose flour
Capers	chopped green olives
Caraway seed	fennel seed or cumin
Cardamom	cinnamon or mace
Chervil	parsley or tarragon or ground anise seed (use a bit less)

Ingredient Called for	Substitute
Chives	onion powder (small amount) or finely chopped leeks or shallots (small amount) or scallion greens
Chocolate, baking, unsweetened	3 tablespoons unsweetened cocoa powder + 1 tablespoon (one ounce or square) butter or 3 tablespoons carob powder + 2 tablespoons water
Chocolate, semisweet (6 ounces)	9 tablespoons unsweetened cocoa powder or squares + 7 tablespoons sugar + 3 tablespoons butter
Cilantro	parsley and lemon juice
Cinnamon	allspice (use less) or cardamom
Cloves (ground)	allspice or nutmeg or mace
Club soda	sparkling mineral water or seltzer
Cornmeal	polenta
Cornstarch	flour, as thickener
Corn syrup, light (1 cup)	1¾ cup granulated sugar + ¼ cup more of the liquid called for in recipe
Crème fraîche	sour cream in a most recipes or ½ sour cream + ½ heavy cream in sauces. Note that crème fraîche can be boiled but sour cream cannot.
Cumin	1 part anise + 2 parts caraway or fennel seed (grind if necessary)

Ingredient Called for	Substitute
Dill seed	caraway or celery seed
Egg (1)	1 tablespoon cornstarch + 3 tablespoons water or 3 tablespoons mayonnaise or ½ of a mashed banana + ¼ teaspoon baking powder
Evaporated milk	half-and-half or cream
Flour	cornstarch or instant potato flakes or pancake mix
Garlic (1 medium clove)	¼ teaspoon minced dried garlic or ⅛ teaspoon garlic powder or ½ teaspoon garlic salt (omitting ½ teaspoon salt from recipe)
Ghee	clarified butter
Herbs, fresh (1 tablespoon)	1 teaspoon dried herbs
Honey (1 cup, in baked goods)	1¼ cups granulated sugar + ¼ cup more of the liquid called for in recipe
Lemongrass	lemon juice or lemon zest or finely chopped lemon verbena or lime zest
Lovage	celery leaves
Marjoram	oregano (use small amount) or thyme or savory
Masa harina	cornmeal
Mascarpone	8 ounces cream cheese whipped with 3 tablespoons sour cream and 2 tablespoons milk

Ingredient Called for	Substitute
Milk (in baked goods)	fruit juice + ½ teaspoon baking soda mixed in with the flour
Milk (1 cup)	½ cup evaporated milk + ½ cup water or ¼ cup powdered milk + ⅞ cup of water Milk, whole same as above + 2 ½ teaspoons melted and cooled butter
Milk, evaporated	half-and-half or cream
Molasses	honey
Nutmeg	allspice or cloves or mace
Oregano	marjoram or thyme
Pancetta	lean bacon (cooked) or very thinly sliced ham
Polenta	cornmeal or corn grits
Poultry seasoning	sage + a blend of any of these: Thyme, marjoram, savory, black pepper, rosemary
Rosemary	thyme
Saffron (⅛ teaspoon)	1 teaspoon dried yellow marigold petals or 1 teaspoon safflower petals
Sage	poultry seasoning or savory or marjoram
Self-rising flour (1 cup)	1 cup all-purpose flour + 1½ teaspoons baking powder + ⅛ teaspoon salt
Shallots	scallions or leeks or yellow onions
Shortening (baked goods only)	butter or margarine

Ingredient Called for	Substitute
Sour cream	1 tablespoon white vinegar + milk (let stand 5 minutes before using) or 1 tablespoon lemon juice + evaporated milk or plain yogurt
Tahini	peanut butter
Tarragon	anise (use small amount) or chervil (use larger amount) or parsley (use larger amount) or a pinch of fennel seed
Tomato paste (1 tablespoon)	1 tablespoon ketchup or ½ cup tomato sauce (reduce some of the liquid in recipe)
Turmeric	mustard powder
Vanilla extract (baked goods only)	almond extract or any other extract
Vinegar	lemon juice for cooking and salads or wine in marinades
Yogurt	sour cream or crème fraîche or buttermilk or mayonnaise (in small amounts)

The Glass Baking Dish Rule

Casseroles and baked goods should always be cooked at the temperature specified in the recipe, with one notable exception: If you are using a glass baking dish, reduce the specified oven temperature by 25°. Glass heats more slowly than metal, but it retains heat well; failing to lower the temperature can result in burned bottoms.

Warped baking pans should always be discarded or repurposed. The uneven surface will spoil the quality of the baked goods.

Greasing the Pan

When you need to grease a baking pan, vegetable shortening is your best option. Butter has a low smoke point and burns easily, and salted butter can cause food to stick to the pan.

Wax Paper Prescription

When braising or stewing meat or poultry, always place a piece of waxed paper under the lid. It will collect the moisture that would otherwise dilute your dish.

Defrosting in the Microwave

If you've ever defrosted meat or fish in the microwave, you probably know that the "defrost" setting or a low power are your best bet for ensuring the outer edges of the food doesn't cook before the middle can defrost. But here's something you might not know: Arranging loose pieces of meat in a single layer with thickest parts or largest pieces toward the outside will also ensure more even defrosting.

Meat Market Primer

Wish you could always pick the most tender cuts of meat? These hints will help. When purchasing a chuck roast, look for white cartilage near the top of the roast. If you can spot a roast with cartilage showing, you've found the first cut, which will be the most tender. When purchasing an eye of round roast, try to find the one that is the same size on both ends. For round steak, look for uneven cuts, which are the ones closest to the sirloin.

Who Knew?

Food that is labeled "no preservatives" means exactly what it says, but don't confuse it with the label "no preservatives added"—this is used to label food that could contain natural preservatives such as salt and essential oils.

Look for Lines

As your probably know, white streaks running through meat are fat. But even if you're diet-conscious, you should always choose well-marbled meat, which indicates that the animal didn't exercise a lot, and the meat will be tender. Fat is a storage depot for energy, and for its meat to be well marbled, an animal must be fed a diet high in rich grains such as corn (which is where we get the old saying that corn-fed beef is best). The fat imparts flavor and provides moisture that helps tenderize the meat.

The Wrapping Is Everything

When choosing meat or poultry in the supermarket, make sure that there is no liquid on the bottom of the package. If there is, it means the food has been frozen and thawed; the cells have ruptured, releasing some of their fluids. To store meat in the refrigerator, wrap it in clean plastic wrap or waxed paper. The supermarket wrapping often contains bloody residues.

Green Ham and Eggs?

Have you ever purchased a ham that has a greenish, glistening sheen? This occasionally occurs when a ham is sliced and the surface is exposed to the effects of oxidation. It isn't a sign of spoilage, but is caused by the nitrite modification of the iron content of the meat, which tends to produce a biochemical change in the meat's pigmentation.

Meat Miracle

All meat (except organ meats and ground beef) should stand at room temperature for a few minutes before cooking. This allows it to brown more evenly, cook faster, retain more juices, and stick less when frying.

● Who Knew? Readers' Favorite

To easily slice meat or poultry thinly, partially freeze it beforehand and your knife will glide right through.

Fish Safety

Seafood is responsible for a lot of food poisoning, but it's perfectly safe and very healthy if treated correctly. If you can't use a fish immediately, remove it from its original wrapping and rinse in cold water. Wrap it loosely in plastic wrap, store in the coldest part of the refrigerator, and use within two days. Store ready-to-eat fish such as smoked mackerel separately from raw fish.

Egg Safety

Eggs have been found to contain the salmonella bacteria even when the shells were not cracked. Because of this, be sure not to use eggs in sauces that are not cooked thoroughly. When preparing a hollandaise or béarnaise sauce, it might be best to microwave the eggs briefly before adding them to the sauce. To do so, first separate the egg yolks completely from the whites (do only two eggs at a time). Then place the two yolks in a glass bowl and beat them until they are well combined. Add 2 teaspoons lemon juice and mix thoroughly again. Now cover the bowl and microwave it on high until you see the surface of the mixture beginning to move. Cook for 10 seconds past this point, remove the bowl, and beat the mixture with a clean whisk or fork until it's smooth. Return the bowl to the microwave and repeat the previous step: Cook 10 seconds past when the surface starts to move, remove, and whisk till smooth. Let the mixture stand (covered) for 1 minute. Your yolks are now free of salmonella, and will still be usable in your sauce!

A Good Temper

When adding raw eggs or yolks to a hot mixture, be sure to mix part of the hot mixture into the eggs, and then gradually add this new mixture to the hot mixture. Called "tempering," it may be extra work, but it makes the eggs less likely to curdle and separate.

Cracks Are Wack

Bacteria love eggs, so if you find a cracked egg in the carton, throw it out; it is probably contaminated. The refrigerator shelf life of eggs is about five weeks from the "sell by" date.

Who Knew?

If your cookbook doesn't specify what size egg to use, go with large eggs. The volume difference in a small egg compared with a large egg can be enough to change the consistency and the quality of the item.

Egg White Wisdom

When beating egg whites for a recipe, remove all traces of yolk from the bowl with a Q-tip or the edge of a paper towel before trying to beat the whites. The slightest trace of yolk will prevent the whites from beating properly, as will any trace of fat on the beaters or bowl.

Washing Winner

When washing vegetables, place a small amount of salt in a sink full of cold water to draw out any sand and insects.

Bag the Baking Soda

You may have heard the old household tip that baking soda added to the cooking water will help vegetables retain their color, but it will also cause them to lose texture and vitamins. To help veggies keep their color, forget the baking soda and simply cook them for no more than 5–7 minutes.

Make It Hot

If you need to add more water to vegetables as they are cooking, make sure the added water is as hot as possible. Adding cold water to already-cooking veggies may affect their cell walls and cause them to toughen.

Carrot Can-Do

If you only have a few carrots to peel, a standard vegetable peeler will get the skins off your carrots quickly and easily. But what if you have a whole bunch of carrots to peel? To slip the skin off carrots in one giant batch, drop them in boiling water, let them stand for 5 minutes, then place them in cold water for a few seconds. The skins will come off easily.

Peeling Potatoes

The easiest way to peel a potato is to boil it first, then drop it into a bowl of ice water for a few seconds to loosen the skin. To keep peeled potatoes white during cooking, add a small amount of white vinegar to the water.

Potato How-To

A new (red) potato has more moisture than other potatoes. Use new potatoes in dishes such as potato salad; they absorb less water when boiled and less mayonnaise when prepared, allowing your salad to have better flavor and less fat. They'll also break apart less easily when you mix the salad. Russet and Yukon gold potatoes are better for baking and making French fries. They are drier, meatier, and starchier, so they have a lighter texture when baked. Their lower water content means the oil will spatter less when you fry them. When baking a potato, make sure you pierce it so steam can escape; otherwise, it may become soggy.

Who Knew?

Sweet potatoes are a root, whereas yams and white potatoes are enlarged stems called tubers that extend underground. The tuber is where the plant stores excess carbohydrates, which is why sweet potatoes are better than "regular" potatoes for those on a low-carb diet.

Cruciferous Cooking

When you cook cruciferous vegetables like broccoli, cabbage, and cauliflower, never use an aluminum or iron pot. The sulfur compounds in the vegetables will react with the metal. For instance, cauliflower will turn yellow if cooked in aluminum, and brown if cooked in iron.

Onions Go First

When sautéing onions and garlic together, be sure to sauté the onions first for at least half of their cooking time. If you start the garlic at the same time as the onions, it will overcook and possibly burn, releasing a chemical that will make the dish bitter.

Creating Caramelized Vegetables

Caramelized vegetables have nothing to do with caramel candy, but they taste almost as good. Caramelizing is the process of oxidizing the sugar content of a vegetable, which produces a sweet, nutty flavor and a brown color. To easily caramelize an onion or other vegetable, toss the slices in extra virgin olive oil and roast them in a 400° oven for 10–30 minutes, or until they're golden brown. You'll love the flavor for stirfrys and on top of pizza.

Pitting Practice

This trick is for adults only: To easily remove an avocado pit, thrust the blade of a sharp knife into the pit, twist slightly, and the pit will come right out.

When It's Good to Add Sugar

Cooking fruit? To make sure it doesn't get mushy, always add sugar to the cooking syrup. The sugar will draw some of the fluid back into the cells to maintain equilibrium in the sugar concentration, and the fruit will retain a more appealing texture.

Frozen Berry Delight

Frozen berries are filled with just as many healthy antioxidants as fresh ones, and in winter they are an excellent source of vitamin C as well as containing small amounts of vitamin A and calcium. If you're not going to enjoy the berries while they're still frozen, thaw them in the refrigerator. The fruit will have time to reabsorb its sugars as it thaws.

Shelling Secret

The easiest way to shell pecans, walnuts, and other nuts? Freeze them first. It shrinks the nut away from the shell, and makes the job a breeze. Another easy way to shell nuts is to soak them in boiling water for 15 minutes.

Grating Soft Cheese?

It's easier to grate Cheddar and other softer cheeses if you place it in the freezer for 10–15 minutes before grating. If the cheese is really soft, don't even bother with the grater. An easier method is to just push the cheese through a colander with a potato masher.

Grater Priorities

Here's a chef's secret for keeping a grater clean so you can use it repeatedly without washing: Simply grate the softest items first, then grate the firmer ones.

The easiest way to clean a cheese grater is to spray it with vegetable oil before grating any cheese, which will make it less sticky. Afterward, rub the crusty heel from a stale loaf of French bread over the dirty end, and your clean-up is finished!

Traveling with Food

When transporting food that can spoil, never put them in the trunk. Always put them in an ice-filled cooler and inside the air-conditioned car. If possible, you shouldn't leave food in a cooler for longer than an hour.

A Last-Ditch Clean for Casserole Dishes

If you've tried everything to clean the caked-on grime on a casserole dish or other oven-proof glassware, try this. Place the glassware in a garbage bag, then cover it with oven cleaner. Tie the bag tightly shut, then leave it outdoors in the sun. When you open it, make sure to keep away from the noxious fumes! Using rubber gloves, wash the dishes in the sink with warm water and dishwashing liquid. They'll be so sparkling, people will think they're new!

CHAPTER 12

Breakfast and Lunch

Who doesn't enjoy an iced coffee on a sultry summer day? To make sure melting ice doesn't dilute your drink, make ice cubes using the small amount of coffee left at the bottom of your coffee pot each morning. Use them in your ice coffee and it will never taste watered down. This is also a great tip for iced tea!

Fresh-Tasting, Reheated Coffee

When you keep coffee warm in a coffeepot on a hot plate, it will only stay fresh for about 30 minutes after it is brewed. If your coffee needs to be freshened up, add a pinch of salt to your cup before reheating it. You won't taste the salt, but your coffee will taste like it's just been brewed.

How to Save Your Cream

If your cream or half-and-half has begun to develop an "off" odor, but you desperately need it for your coffee, try mixing in ⅛ teaspoon of baking soda, which will neutralize the lactic acid that is causing the souring in the cream. Before you use the cream, however, taste it to be sure the flavor is still acceptable.

The Most Important Meal of the Day

For a quick and healthy breakfast, make waffles and pancakes ahead of time, then freeze them. When you or your family is ready to eat, pop them in the toaster to reheat. Making waffles from scratch, rather than buying them in the frozen foods section, will also save you money.

For Sweeter Grapefruit

It's surprising, but true: A small amount of salt will make a grapefruit taste sweeter.

Breakfast Bar Saver

Don't have time to eat anything but a breakfast bar in the morning? Store it in a glasses case to make sure it doesn't get smushed in your purse or bag on the way to work.

Toasty Treat

For a different type of toast, lightly butter a slice of bread on both sides and cook it in a waffle iron. Your kids will love it!

● Who Knew?

White and brown eggs are identical in nutritional value and taste. Believe it or not, the only difference is that white eggs come from white chickens, and brown eggs come from brown chickens!

With Eggs, Your Bowl Matters

Aluminum bowls and cookware tend to darken eggs. The reason? The aluminum's chemical reaction with the egg protein. If you happen to have one, always use a copper bowl when beating eggs. The copper will release ions during the beating process that cause the protein in the whites to become more stable. The next best material to use is stainless steel; however, you will need to add a pinch of cream of tartar to stabilize the whites. Whatever bowl you choose, make sure it has a rounded bottom to ensure that all the mixture comes into contact with the mixing blades or your fork.

Save Your Yolks

Believe it or not, you can save egg yolks for later use. If you have used egg whites in a recipe and want to save the yolks, slide them into a bowl of water, cover with plastic wrap, and store in the refrigerator for a day or two. It beats throwing them out!

Poaching Eggs

The fresher the egg, the better it is for poaching. The white will be firmer and will help to keep the yolk from breaking. Salt, lemon juice, and vinegar will make egg whites coagulate faster. Add a dash of one of these ingredients to the water when you're poaching eggs to help them keep their shape.

Sunny Side Secrets

When frying an egg, the butter or margarine should be very hot before the eggs are added—a drop of water should sizzle. However, the heat should be reduced just before the eggs are added to the pan. Cook the eggs over low heat until the whites are completely set. Add a couple drops of water and cover the pan just before the eggs are done to get a perfect white film over the yolks.

Soft-boiled eggs should be cooked at least four minutes to kill any bacteria that may be present. The whites of fried eggs should be hard, although the yolks may be soft. Eggs are considered safe at 160°F.

For the Best-Ever Omelet

To make a great omelet, be sure the eggs are at room temperature (take them out of the fridge 30 minutes beforehand). Cold eggs are too stiff to make a fluffy omelet. For a super fluffy omelet, add ½ teaspoon baking soda for every three eggs. Also, try adding a pinch of water instead of milk. The water increases the volume of the eggs at least three times more than the milk does. The coagulated proteins hold in the liquid, resulting in a moist omelet.

Easy Egg Clean-Up

Cleaning up after a yummy scrambled egg breakfast? Cold water cleans egg off pans and utensils better than hot water. Hot water tends to cause the protein to bind to surfaces and harden.

Pancake Secrets

Short-order cooks and chefs have a host of tricks to make the lightest pancakes. Here are a few we've learned:

✦ Don't overmix the batter—you don't want the gluten in the flour to overdevelop and allow the carbon dioxide that makes the little air pockets to escape. It's better to leave a couple of lumps in the batter.

✦ Refrigerate the batter for up to 30 minutes. This further slows the development of the gluten and the leavening action.

✦ Always stir the batter before you pour it onto the griddle. The ingredients can settle; stirring recombines them and aerates the batter.

✦ Make sure you flip pancakes as soon as air bubbles appear on the top, then flip them back over if necessary to finish cooking them. If you wait until the bubbles break, gas escapes, and your pancakes won't be as light or fluffy.

✦ If you like brown-on-the-outside pancakes, add a little extra sugar. The sugar caramelizes, giving a browner color to the pancakes. Also, some people swear by adding a tablespoon of pure maple syrup (the real stuff—no imitations!) into your pancake batter.

✦ For perfectly formed pancakes, use a meat baster to squeeze the batter onto the griddle. It gives you so much control you'll finally be able to make those animal-shaped pancakes your kids have been begging you for!

Key to a Clean Griddle

When cooking on the griddle, you'll get better results if you clean it between each batch of pancakes or whatever you happen to be making. Do this easily with coarse salt wrapped in a piece of cheesecloth. The salt will provide a light abrasive cleaning and won't harm the surface if you're gentle.

Test Your Griddle

Pancakes and other griddle treats often require a precise temperature to cook to their best. But how do you know when it's reached the right temperature? Flick a few drops of water on the heated griddle. If the surface is 325° (the perfect temperature for pancakes), the droplets will skitter and dance—steam causes the drops to rise, but gravity brings them back down. If the griddle is 425°F or hotter, the water drops will be propelled right off the griddle.

Who Knew? Readers' Favorite

Here's a trick to keep waffles from sticking to the waffle iron: Beat a teaspoon of white wine into the batter. You'll never taste the wine, but it will keep the batter from adhering to the hot surface.

Syrup Substitute

Out of maple syrup and wanted to make waffles this morning? Make this delicious substitute. Combine ⅓ cup butter, ⅓ cup sugar, and ½ cup frozen orange juice in a saucepan. Cook over medium heat, stirring constantly, until the sugar has dissolved and the mixture is syrupy.

Splattering Solution

If bacon were still produced the old-fashioned way, by curing it slowly and using a dry salt, it would not splatter when cooked. Today's bacon is cured in brine, which speeds up the curing process. The additional liquid from the brine gets released when the bacon is cooked, causing the fat to splatter. To reduce splattering, use a low heat setting. This will also reduce the number of nitrites that convert into carcinogens, because high heat tends to convert the nitrites faster than does lower heat. To reduce splattering, you can also soak the bacon in ice-cold water for 2–4 minutes, and then dry it well with paper towels before frying it. Or try sprinkling the bacon with a bit of flour before cooking it.

Bacon Wrapper

If you're cooking less than a full package of bacon, how do you store the extra slices? Just roll each slice into a tight cylinder, place in an airtight plastic bag, and freeze. Simply thaw and unroll when you're ready to cook!

Stop Sausage Splitting

Keep sausages from splitting when cooking them by piercing the skin in one or two places while they are cooking. Rolling them in flour before cooking will reduce shrinkage.

Soggy Lunch?

If your kids complain that the sandwiches you make in the morning are mushy by lunchtime, put the mayonnaise (or any condiment) in an resealable plastic bag, and stick it in the lunch box. This way, the kids can season their own sandwiches at lunchtime by turning the bag inside out and rubbing it on the bread.

Lunchbox Lesson

Freezing juice boxes is an excellent way to make sure your child's juice will still be cold at lunchtime, as well as keeping everything else in the lunchbox cool.

Be Prepared

Make school-day mornings a little less crazy by preparing a few days' worth of the kids' sandwiches at the same time (without condiments),

 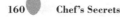

then freezing them. Each morning, just toss the pre-made sandwich in their lunch boxes, add a small container or plastic bag with the condiments, and by lunchtime, the bread will have thawed and become soft and fresh-tasting.

Forget About Refreezing

When any type of meat or lunchmeat is refrozen, the fat content may cause the food to become rancid. And this is only one reason why meats should not be frozen again after they've been thawed—the texture of the meat can suffer, and improper thawing can promote bacterial growth. Instead, refrigerate leftover meats, which can be stored safely for four days.

Stab that Potato!

When baking potatoes, pierce the skin with a fork to allow the steam to escape. Your reward will be a wonderfully fluffy texture.

Oil, Not Foil, for Baked Potatoes

Many people wrap a potato in foil thinking that it will speed up the baking time. A faster method is to rub the skin lightly with vegetable oil.

Quick Quiche Tip

Quiches, especially those made with onions and mushrooms, should not be allowed to cool. Both of these vegetables have a high water content, which will be released into the quiche as it cools. The result: A soggy crust and runny filling. If buying a pre-made quiche, look for ones that don't have onions or mushrooms, and when making your own, make sure to serve after letting it sit for 10 minutes (which will prevent oozing).

Who Knew?

Never set pans next to each other on the same oven rack. Air space between pans is important because the hot air needs to circulate.

Less Gas, More Beans

You don't have to avoid baked beans because you fear they'll make you gassy. Instead, just add a dash or two of baking soda to the beans when they're cooking, and their gas-producing properties will be dramatically reduced.

For the Best Fries Around

For the greatest French fries, soak cut potatoes in ice-cold water in the refrigerator for an hour; this will harden them so that they absorb less fat. Dry them thoroughly, then fry them twice. First cook them for 6–7 minutes, drain them well, and then sprinkle them lightly with flour (this step makes them extra crispy and crunchy). Then fry them again for 1–2 minutes, until they are golden brown.

Warm Sandwiches

Who doesn't love a warm sandwich? Luckily, you don't need an expensive sandwich press to make delicious heated sandwiches—just use your microwave! When heating a sandwich in the microwave, you'll get the best results using firm, textured bread such as French or sourdough. The filling should be heated separately. If the filling is heated in the sandwich, be sure to spread it evenly over the bread and very close to the edges. Wait a few minutes before eating the sandwich, as the filling may remain very hot even if the bread is cool to the touch.

Salting Solution

Salt homemade potato chips by putting them in a paper bag with salt and shaking. This way, the salt is evenly distributed—and the paper absorbs the excess grease. Save calories wherever you can!

Ring Around the Onion Ring

Cooking onion rings? Make sure you fry only a few at a time. This prevents them from sticking together and ensures even cooking.

Make Canned Soups Better

If you feel like canned soups are bland or watery, but still want the convenience, try substituting broth for the water you would normally add to the pot. Not surprisingly, chicken broth goes well with chicken soups, and beef for beef-based ones. But beef broth also goes great with tomato soup, and vegetable broth can be added to anything. For even better flavor, add a dried bay leaf when you add the broth.

To help a semisolid or condensed soup slide right out of the can, shake the can first, and then open it from the bottom.

Tomato Soup Tip

Cream-of-tomato soup can be tricky to make from scratch. To keep it from curdling, the order in which you add the ingredients matters: Add the tomato base to the milk instead of the milk to the tomato. Stirring a small amount of flour into the milk also helps.

A Smoother Finish for Soups

When serving creamed soups from the can, beat or whisk for 10–15 seconds before heating and your soup will be silky smooth.

Salad Starter

Who doesn't love perfect carrot peels on the top of salads? Getting this great look is easy. Just peel off slices of carrot with a vegetable peeler, then drop them into a bowl of ice water.

Quickie Salad Dressing

If you want to make a quick and unique salad dressing, just place a small amount of olive oil and wine vinegar inside an almost-empty ketchup bottle. Shake it up and drizzle over your salad. Voilà!

Salad Saver

For the crispiest salad, prepare it in a metal bowl and then place it in the freezer for one minute before serving.

Soggy Salad Be Gone!

Avoid wet, limp salads by placing an inverted saucer in the bottom of the salad bowl before you throw in all your veggies. The excess water that is left after washing the vegetables and greens will drain under the saucer and leave the greens high and dry.

Hard-Boiled How-To

Who doesn't love a hard-boiled egg? Great for snacks or a light lunch, these tasty treats are easy to prepare—especially with our hard-boiled-egg tips and tricks.

✦ You can prevent boiled eggs from cracking by using lemon. Just cut a lemon in half, then rub the cut side on the shells before cooking them. You can also add a pinch of salt to the water before to prevent cracks.

✦ If an egg does crack during boiling, remove it from the water and, while it is still wet, pour a generous amount of salt over the crack. Let the egg stand for 20 seconds, then put it back into the boiling water.

✦ Boiled eggs should be cooled at room temperature before refrigerating them.

✦ To easily remove the shell from a hard-boiled egg in one piece, exert gentle pressure while rolling it around on the counter, then insert a teaspoon between the shell and the egg white and rotate it.

✦ Always cool a hard-boiled egg before you try to slice it; it will slice more easily and won't fall apart. Your best implement if you don't have an egg-slicer? Using unwaxed dental floss makes slicing hard-cooked eggs easy.

✦ Using your hard-boiled eggs for egg salad? The fastest way to chop eggs is to peel them, place them in a bowl, and run a pizza cutter through them several times.

Who Knew?

Never eat an egg with a silver spoon. Not only will the spoon tarnish more quickly, but the reaction of the egg and the silver can leave a foul taste in your mouth.

CHAPTER 13

Dinner

For the Best Roasted Chicken and Turkey

Who doesn't love chicken and turkey? Poultry is not only a popular choice for dinner, it's also inexpensive! Make cooking chicken and turkey in the oven easier with these tips.

✦ Chickens and turkeys must be thoroughly cleaned inside and out before cooking, in order to remove any residue that may be left from the slaughtering process. If you detect a slight "off" odor when you open the package, rinse the bird under cool water, then submerge in a solution of water plus 1 tablespoon lemon juice or vinegar and 1 teaspoon salt per cup of water. Refrigerate 1–4 hours before cooking.

✦ Try basting the bird with a small amount of white zinfandel or vermouth—it will help crisp the skin, and the sugar in the drink imparts a brown color and glaze to the outside of the meat. Or, brush the skin with reduced-sodium soy sauce during the last 30 minutes to produce a beautiful brown color.

✦ A chicken or turkey cooked at a constant 375° will be juicier because more fat and moisture will be retained.

✦ Have a V-rack? Try cooking your next bird breast-side down on the V-rack for the first hour. The juices will flow to the breast and make the meat moist and tender. Remove the V-rack after the first hour. After trying this, you will never buy another commercially prepared self-basting bird!

- If your roasted chicken or turkey tends to be too dry, try stuffing a whole apple inside the bird before roasting. (Just toss the apple afterward.) You can also line the bottom of the pan with lemon and onion slices. They'll give the bird a lovely flavor and make sure it stays moist.

- For the most tender bird you've ever eaten, try submerging the chicken or turkey in buttermilk and refrigerating for two to three hours before cooking.

- Once poultry has finished cooking, it should be allowed to rest for about 20 minutes before carving. As with other roasts, this standing time allows the proteins in the meat to reabsorb the juices, so they stay in the meat rather than spilling onto the cutting board.

● Who Knew?

To prevent the growth of bacteria, cooked poultry should never remain at room temperature for more than 40 minutes. If you've stuffed the bird, remove the stuffing immediately.

Dark Versus Light

Cooking chicken breasts with the ribs intact tends to keep the meat moister. But if you're cooking chicken parts separately, remember that dark meat takes longer to cook than white does because of its higher fat content. Start the dark meat a few minutes before the white. The white meat might be too dry if it is cooked as long as the dark.

Skinning a Bird?

The easiest way to skin poultry is to partially freeze it first. The skin will come right off the bird with almost no effort.

Stock-Making Secrets

One mistake people frequently make when preparing stock is to place soup bones in the water after it has come to a boil. This tends to seal the bone and prevent all the flavor and nutrients from being released into the stock! The bone should be added to the cold water when the pot is first placed on the stove. This will allow the maximum release of flavors, nutrients, and especially the gelatinous thickening agents that add body to the stock.

Do-It-Yourself Bouillon Cubes

Make your own bouillon cubes by freezing leftover chicken broth in ice-cube trays. Once frozen, the cubes can be kept frozen in resealable plastic bags until needed. They are easily defrosted in the microwave—or just toss them into a soup or sauce, and they'll melt quickly.

The Best Breaded Breasts

Always refrigerate chicken breasts after flouring, but before cooking. The coating will adhere better that way. Also, try adding a teaspoon of baking powder to your batter, and using club soda instead of water for a delicate coating.

Common Sense Breading

When breading chicken cutlets, make sure you don't bread your fingers, too, by always using one hand for wet ingredients and the other for the breadcrumbs.

A three-pound chicken will yield about 2½ cups of meat, or five servings.

For Super-Tender Pork

When roasting a pork loin, cook it with the fat-side down for the first 20 minutes. This will cause the fat to begin to liquefy. Then turn the roast over for the balance of the cooking time, and the fat will baste the meat.

Ham Purchasing Secrets

If you're going to buy a canned ham, purchase the largest one you can afford. Most smaller canned hams are made from bits and pieces glued together with gelatin. Cured hams are injected with a solution of brine salts, sugar, and nitrites. The weight of the ham will increase with the injection, and if the total weight goes up by 8 percent, the label will usually say "ham with natural juices." If the weight of the ham increases by more than 10 percent, the label must read "water added."

Perfectly Sliced Ham

If ham is on the menu, ask your butcher to slice it when you buy it. When it's time to cook, just secure the ham with dental floss, and bake as usual. When it's done, you won't have to slice it, and the slices will look perfect. Slicing it ahead of time will also allow the glaze to seep into the ham a little farther.

For Less Salty Ham

To make your ham less salty, pour a can of ginger ale over it, then rub the meaty side with salt at least an hour before baking it. This will cause the saltwater in the meat to come to the surface, which will reduce the saltiness of the ham.

Ham Bone Help

To easily remove a ham bone, slit the ham lengthwise down to the bone before placing it in the pan—but leave the bone in the ham. While the ham is baking, the meat will pull away and the bone will come out easily after the ham is cooked. Leaving the bone in will also lead to moister meat.

"Shanks" for the Tip

When purchasing a lamb shank, be sure it weighs at least 3 pounds. If the shank is any smaller, the percentage of bone will be too high in relation to the amount of meat.

Moister Meatloaf

When you are preparing meat loaf, try rubbing the top and sides with a small amount of water instead of tomato sauce. This will stop the meat loaf from cracking and drying out as it cooks—and who wants a dried out meat loaf? If you like a tomato flavor, add tomato sauce 15 minutes before the meat is fully cooked.

Hamburger Helpers

If you are preparing hamburger (or meatloaf) with very low-fat meat, mix in one well-beaten egg white for every pound of meat. This will give it a richer flavor without adding a lot of fat. Add a package of instant onion-soup mix to a pound of meat for tons of flavor, and mix in some cottage cheese or instant potatoes to keep it moist and make less meat feed more people!

Easy-Greasy

If you wet your hands with cold water before shaping sausage or hamburger patties, the grease won't stick to your fingers.

No More So-So Leftovers

When you refrigerate cooked beef, its fat oxidizes quickly, which will often give day-old burgers an "off" taste. If you know you'll be eating tonight's meal tomorrow as well, discourage fat oxidization by not cooking the beef in iron or aluminum pots and pans, and not salting the meat until you are ready to eat it.

Market Watch

Supermarkets have started using their own wording on meat packages to make you think the meat you are buying is a better grade than it really is. Most of the major chains are buying more select-grade beef, but may call it by a number of fancy names such as "top premium beef," "prime quality cut," "select choice," "market choice," or "premium cut." Be aware that these titles don't actually mean anything!

Beef Up the Dark

The best-tasting beef should be a dark red color with slightly yellowish fat. If the fat is too white or the meat is bright red, the beef hasn't been hung for long enough and will be lower on taste and tougher. It's better if there's some fat marbled throughout, as this makes it more tender.

Who Knew? Readers' Favorite

Want the fastest way to make meatballs? Well here it is! Shape the meat mixture into a log and then cut off slices, which then rolls easily into balls.

Meatballs for Health

When eating pasta, try to balance the meal with some protein. This will allow the blood-sugar levels to be normalized. Maybe that's why Grandma always made meatballs with spaghetti!

Moister Meatballs

If you insert a small piece of cracked ice into the center of your meatballs before browning them, they will be moister. But be careful—you'll need to experiment to make sure the centers don't remain raw. Cut open a meatball and check the doneness of the center to determine the proper browning time.

When Should You Season A Steak?

The jury's still out on when in the cooking process you should season a steak. One authority says to salt before cooking, another equally respected one says to salt after cooking. If you salt before, you get the benefit of a nice salty flavor through-and-through, but the salt tends to draw liquid from the meat, so make sure you're replenishing its juices. Whether you decide to salt before or after, you should never use ground pepper on any meat that is to be cooked in a pan with dry heat. Pepper tends to become bitter when scorched by the heat of a dry pan.

Press for Doneness

When cooking steak, it's good to know that the internal temperature of a rare steak is 135° F, medium-rare is 145° F, medium is 160° F, and well done is 170° F. However, an experienced chef rarely uses a thermometer when cooking a steak. Meat has a certain resiliency, and the experienced chef can just press the steak with a finger to tell whether the meat is rare, medium-rare, medium, medium-well, or well done. As meat cooks it loses water, and the more it cooks, the firmer it becomes. Try pressing on your steaks to get a feel for how they feel at different stages of doneness, and you'll never need to cut them open to find out again.

● Who Knew?

You'll often hear someone refer to a rare steak as "bloody," but in reality, the blood is drained at slaughterhouses and hardly any ever remains in the meat. The red juice you see is actually the result of a pigment called myoglobin, which is found in the muscles of all meat.

Against the Grain

Here's a simple tip to make your meat more tender. When it's ready to slice, make sure to cut it against the grain (look for slight lines on the surface). Meat cut across the grain will be more tender.

A Great Use for Stale Bread

If you're broiling steaks or chops, save a few slices of stale, dried bread and set them in the bottom of the broiler pan to absorb fat drippings. This will eliminate smoking fat, and it should also reduce any danger of a grease fire.

Let the Air Flow for Roasts

Always use a shallow pot for cooking roasts. This will allow air to circulate more efficiently. Elevating the meat by cooking it atop celery ribs, carrot sticks, thick onion slices also helps get the air underneath the meat (and give it a great flavor!).

Timing Roasts

Don't have a roasting chart nearby? Then follow this rule of thumb: Beef roasts will take about 20 minutes for the first pound and about 15 minutes for every pound thereafter. The USDA recommends cooking beef to an internal temperature of at least 145° F.

To Cover or Not to Cover, That Is the Question

The two methods normally used for cooking a roast are dry heat (without liquid) or moist heat (with liquid). When the meat is covered, steam is trapped in the pan. Many cooks use this method to prevent the roast from drying out. Dry heat (with the lid off) will brown the outside of the roast, and, if you wish, you can baste it every 15 minutes to provide the desired moisture. If you go the moist heat route, lower the temperature by 25°F, and make sure to turn the roast or cook it on a rack so its underside won't get mushy.

Let the Roast Rest

Let a roast stand at room temperature for about 15 minutes before you carve it. This gives the juices time to be reabsorbed and evenly distributed. When you cook a roast, the juices tend to be forced to the center as those near the surface get evaporated by the heat. Resting the roast also allows the meat to firm up a bit, making it easier to carve into thinner slices.

The Way of Warm Meat

Meat gets tougher as it cools on your plate, because the collagen, which has turned to a tender gelatin, thickens. The best way to eliminate this problem is to be sure you serve steak on a warmed or metal plate. After carving a roast, keep it in a warmer or put it back in the oven and leave the door ajar.

Perfect Leftovers

When storing a cooked roast in the fridge, place it back into its own juices whenever possible. When reheating the sliced meat, place it in a casserole dish with lettuce leaves between each of the slices. The lettuce provides just the right amount of moisture to keep the slices from drying out.

Sauté with Sugar

Before sautéing meats, sprinkle a tiny amount of sugar on the surface of the meat. The sugar will react with the juices and then caramelize, causing a deeper browning as well as improving the flavor.

Tenderizing Trick

To tenderize tough meat without tenderizer, use baking soda. Just rub baking soda all over the meat, refrigerate for a few hours, and rinse well before cooking. For extra tenderizing, cover the meat with slices of kiwi.

Who Knew? Readers' Favorite

Wine corks (the natural kind, not plastic) contain a chemical that, when heated, will help tenderize beef stew. Just throw in 3 or 4 corks while cooking your stew, and don't tell anyone your secret!

You Can't Spell "Tender" without "T"

The tannic acid in strong black tea can tenderize meat in a stew, as well as reduce the cooking time. Just add ½ cup strong tea to the stew when you add the other liquid. It will also give your stew a great brown color.

Let Stews Sit

The perfect "left-over" meal, stews are usually best prepared a day in advance to allow the flavors to blend—or, as the romantic French say, marry.

Stew's Secret Ingredient

Cooking a lamb or beef stew? Add a few tablespoons of black coffee and your stew will have a nice dark color and a rich taste that may become your secret ingredient. This also works well for gravies.

Quick Thickeners

An easy method of thickening stews, soups, or creamed vegetables is to add a small amount of quick-cooking oats, a grated potato, or some instant mashed potatoes. Never add flour directly, as it will clump. But if you're a particularly prepared cook, you can combine a stick of melted butter with ½ cup flour, then place it in a covered bowl in the refrigerator and let it harden. Then when you want a thickener, simply add some of this special mixture. It melts easily and will thicken without lumps.

For Tender, Tasty Chili

Marinate the meat for your chili in beer. It's a great tenderizer for tough, inexpensive cuts of beef, and it will add great flavor. All you need to do is soak the meat for an hour before cooking, or marinate it overnight in the refrigerator.

Seasoning Removal Remedies

Here's a great tip when cooking with whole garlic cloves that you plan to remove before the dish is served: Stick a toothpick firmly in the garlic so it will be easy to take out. Put herbs that fall apart during cooking in a tea infuser to make them easy to remove.

Who Knew?

For the best results and to keep the flavors intact, soups and stews should only simmer, never boil.

Perfectly Brown Gravy

Nineteenth century cooks added onion skins to the gravy while it cooked to give it a brown color, and you can, too! Just make sure you remove the skins after a few minutes and discard. This trick also works for soups and stock.

The Goods on Gravy

If you're like most people, you probably use flour or corn starch to thicken gravy. Because flour thickens somewhat slowly, make sure you don't use too much! Gravy thickens as it cools, so using too much flour can cause it to become a little unappealing by the time you're ready for seconds. It can also taste "floury" rather than having the flavor of the meat juices it's made with. To dispense with the flour entirely, deglaze your roasting pan with water, then add a small amount of butter before reducing the mixture over high heat, stirring frequently, until it is the right consistency.

It's in the (Fish) Eyes

If you're buying fresh fish whole, look at the eyes, which should be clear, and the gills, which should be transparent and bright red in color. Don't be afraid to ask the fishmonger to show you the fish close up—they might give you a fresher fish if they think you know what you're looking for!

Tipping the Scales

If you're gutsy enough to scale your own fish, rub white vinegar on the scales, and then let the fish sit for about 10 minutes and they'll rub right off. Put the fish in a large plastic bag first (hold it by the tail) to keep the scales from flying all over your kitchen.

Get Rid of Fishy Smells

Before handling fish, rub your hands with lemon juice and you won't smell of fish for the rest of the day! After frying fish, put a little white vinegar into the frying pan to help get rid of the odor on the surface.

Testing Fish for Doneness

To test fish for doneness, insert a thin-bladed knife into the flesh at the thickest part. If it's done, it will be just barely translucent in the center. Even though it might look not quite done, the fish will continue to cook after you remove it from the heat, so make sure not to overcook it.

Quick Fish Trick

If you're grilling or broiling thick fish steaks, marinate them for 15 minutes in lemon or lime juice before cooking. The acid from the juice "cooks" the flesh on the fish a bit, cutting down on the time it needs to stay on the heat—so your fish is less likely to dry out.

Cornflake Your Fish

For added crunch with fewer calories, use cornflakes instead of breadcrumbs to coat fish fillets. Not only do cornflakes contain fewer calories than breadcrumbs, they are less absorbent and give a lighter covering, so the fish will absorb less oil.

Dry Fish Fries Better

When frying fish, be sure the surface of the fish is dry before putting it in the oil. Moisture can cool the oil down and make the fish cook less evenly.

Quick and Easy Fish

Our favorite way to prepare fish is also super quick and tasty. Wrap your fillets individually in foil, adding a bit of chopped onion, salt and pepper, and a spring of dill. Bake for 30 minutes in a 350° oven, then unwrap for a tender, flavorful fish.

Frozen Fish Fix

Pining for fresh fish but stuck with frozen? Try this: Cover the frozen fish in milk until it thaws, then cook. It will taste fresher and your family will never know it was frozen.

How to Steam Fish in the Microwave

To steam fish fillets in the microwave, place them in a shallow microwavable dish (a glass pie plate is ideal) with the thinner parts overlapping at the center of the dish. Sprinkle with lemon juice or herbs, if you like, and then cover the dish with plastic wrap (making sure it doesn't touch the fish) and cook for 3 minutes per pound. If your microwave doesn't have a turntable, rotate the dish about halfway through the cooking time.

River fish have more flavor than lake fish because they must swim against currents and thus get more exercise. Fish from cooler waters also have a higher fat content and, therefore, more flavor.

Serving Fish

Fish tends to cool very quickly, so it's best served on warm plates or a warmed platter. Garnish your fish with a wedge of lemon or other citrus.

All About Anchovies

You can reduce the saltiness of anchovies by soaking them in ice water for about 15 minutes. Because of their high salt content, anchovies will keep about two months under refrigeration after the can is opened, and up to a year without refrigeration in a sealed can. Once opened, they should be kept covered with olive oil.

Everything You Need to Know for Delicious Shrimp

Shrimp is low in fat, delicious, and one of the most inexpensive kinds of shellfish you can buy. For the most tender shrimp, cool them down before cooking. Either place them in the freezer for 10–15 minutes, or set them in a bowl of ice water for about 5 minutes. If you're boiling them, drop them into boiling broth or court bouillon for one minute, and then turn off the heat and let stand for 10 minutes. Sautéed shrimp are done when they are firm and pink, which takes 3–5 minutes. Grilled shrimp cook in about seven minutes. No matter how you're cooking them, shrimp cook fast! So make sure to keep a close eye on them. As soon as they turn pink, they're done. (If they are already pink when you purchase them, they've already been cooked, and all you have to do is heat them up.) To make sure you don't overheat shrimp, plunge them in cold water once they've turned pink to immediately stop the cooking process.

Full and Frozen

Frozen shrimp can make for a quick and easy meal, but try to avoid shrimp that has been peeled and deveined before freezing, which usually causes a loss of texture and flavor.

For Lobster You'll Love

It might sound crazy, but the taste, texture, and color of microwaved lobster is far superior to boiled or steamed, and microwaving produces an evenly cooked, tender lobster. Unfortunately, you can only cook one lobster at a time, so put your oven on the lowest heat and use it to keep already-cooked lobsters until your meal is done. To microwave a lobster, place it in a large, microwavable plastic bag with ¼ cup water, and knot the bag loosely. A 1½ pound lobster should take 5–6 minutes on high, providing you have a 600–700 watt microwave. If you have a lower wattage oven, allow about eight minutes. To be sure the lobster is fully cooked, separate the tail from the body. The tail meat should be creamy white, not translucent. Even when microwaved, the lobster must still be cooked live because of the enzymatic breakdown that occurs immediately upon its death. If you are bothered by the lobster's movements, put it in the freezer for 10 minutes before cooking to dull its senses; the movement will be reduced to about 20 seconds.

Eating a Lobster

If you're eating a whole lobster and bibs aren't really your thing, cover the lobster with a napkin or towel before twisting off the legs and claws. This will keep the juices from squirting out and causing a mess.

Crayfish Know-How

Like lobsters and crabs, crayfish are always cooked live. Also known as crawfish or sometimes crawdads, they have a much sweeter flavor than either lobsters or crabs, and all its meat is found in its tail. To remove the meat easily, gently twist the tail away from the body, then unwrap the first three sections of the shell to expose the meat. Next, pinch the end of the meat in one hand while holding the tail in the other, and pull the meat out in one piece. You can also suck out the flavorful juices from the head. Yum!

Opening Shellfish

Cooking shellfish at home can be a lot of fun (not to mention, delicious), so don't be intimidated by the task of opening the shells! To open shellfish, wash the shells thoroughly. Hold the clam or oyster in your palm and slip the tip of an oyster or butter knife between the upper and lower shells. Run the knife around the edge of the shell and pry until you hear a pop at the hinge. Loosen the clam or oyster from the shell and remove any shell fragments.

● Who Knew?

Saturated fat accounts for only 10–25 percent of the total fat in seafood, while it comprises an average of 42 percent of the fat in beef and pork.

Oyster Answers

Store live oysters in the refrigerator in a single layer with the larger shell down, covered with a damp towel. Eat them within two days of purchase. Oysters are easy to overcook, which will make them tough. If you are poaching oysters, take them out as soon as their edges start to curl.

Mussel Madness

Mussels are a succulent seafood treat, and they're not hard to make. Here are some tips to make delicious mussels.

✦ When purchasing, make sure they're alive by tapping their shells. If they're alive, their shells will snap closed. Any mussels that don't close their shells are probably dead and shouldn't be eaten.

✦ Live mussels will keep in the refrigerator for two to three days if placed on a tray and covered with a damp towel. Spread them out; never pile the mussels on top of one another.

✦ Mussels should be cleaned with a stiff brush under cold running water, and if any non-clear liquid comes out, they should be discarded. Remove their visible "beard" just before cooking. Once they have been debearded, mussels will die.

✦ To cook mussels, all you have to do is boil them in a pot. Mussels are cooked when their shells open, and any mussels that aren't open should be discarded. Serve over pasta or with French fries, and enjoy!

The most effective way to get rid of sand and grit from clams is to soak them in water with a bit of cornmeal stirred in. It irritates the clams, and they expel the sand while trying to eliminate the cornmeal.

Clam-Cooking Know-How

The shells of healthy clams should be closed when you buy them, and will gradually open as the clams cook. (If you keep the clams on ice, they will also probably relax and open their shells.) Like mussels, if a clam's shell doesn't open by itself when the clam is cooked, it should be discarded.

Prevent a Clam Calamity

Once clams are dug up, they must be cleansed of sand and debris. To accomplish this, the clams should be allowed to soak in the refrigerator in a solution of 1 part salt to 10 parts water for several hours or overnight. If you're pressed for time, rinse them in a bowl of fresh water, changing it frequently, until no sand remains.

The Truth About Clam Chowder

Chefs always add clams to their chowder during the last 15–20 minutes of cooking. If they are added too early, clams can become either tough or too soft. To retain its flavor, lobster is another meat that should not be added to dishes until just before serving. Overcooking will destroy its taste.

Fluffy Rice How-To

If you like dry, fluffy rice, try this trick as soon as the rice is done cooking: Wrap the lid with a cotton dishtowel and set it on the pot for about 15 minutes. The cloth will absorb the steam.

● Who Knew?

Unless the instructions explicitly direct you to rinse rice before cooking, don't—most rice sold in the United States is coated with a fine powder that contains the B vitamins thiamine and niacin. If you rinse the rice, you wash these nutrients down the drain.

Secrets for Perfect Mashed Potatoes

No matter how long we spend cooking a delicious cut of meat, the mashed potatoes always go faster at our dinner table. Here are some of our favorite tips for perfect mashed potatoes.

✦ Never pour cold milk into cooked potatoes. It will change the taste of the starch, giving it an unpleasant flavor, not unlike cardboard. The milk should be warmed in a pan (preferably with a small amount of garlic or chives for flavor) before being added.

✦ Buttermilk will give the potatoes a great flavor. If you're watching your weight, save some of the cooking water from the potatoes and use that instead of butter or cream.

+ A pinch or two of baking powder will give mashed potatoes extra fluff. Never put baking soda in potatoes; it will turn them black.

+ Never overmix or overcook potatoes. The cell walls will rupture, releasing an excess of starch and resulting in gluey potatoes. Potatoes should be mashed with a vertical motion, not stirred in a circular motion, to minimize the damage that occurs by crushing the cells on the wall of the bowl.

+ Try adding powdered milk or instant potato flakes for extra-fluffy mashed potatoes.

+ Try squeezing some fresh lemon juice into your mashed potatoes instead of butter or oil. Season with freshly ground black pepper for a no-added-fat mash that is flavorful and goes fantastically well with roast chicken.

Pasta Perfection

Cook pasta only until it is slightly chewy (what the Italians call *al dente*, or "to the tooth"). Always use plenty of water, and keep the water at a rapid boil—the pasta needs to move around as it cooks, to keep it from sticking together. Some cooks like to salt the water, but we find it tends to toughen pasta. Use a pinch of sugar instead, and salt just before serving. After it's cooked, don't rinse pasta. Sauce will cling better, and the noodles will retain more nutrients.

Stuffing Secrets

+ Never stuff a turkey or other fowl and leave it overnight, even in the refrigerator. Cooking the bird may not kill all the bacteria, and hundreds of cases of food poisoning occur every year because birds are stuffed and then left for too long before roasting.

✦ If you plan to cook your stuffing in the turkey, consider this tip: Pack it into a piece of cheesecloth before placing it in the bird. When you're ready to remove the stuffing, simply pull the cheesecloth out, and none of the stuffing will be stuck inside the turkey. You can also seal the opening of the bird with a slice of raw potato.

✦ If the stuffing inside the bird is never enough (or if your family picks at the turkey and trimmings before the meal is served), try this. Fill some buttered muffin pans with additional stuffing and bake in a very hot oven. You'll have a stuffing treat that's crunchy on the outside and moist on the inside. Yum!

Lentils Done Easily

Lentils are delicious, and great for you! When cooking them, make sure to add a few teaspoons of oil. It will prevents the pot from spilling over, and actually helps in the cooking process.

A Bean Bonanza

Beans are as delicious as they are nutritious. Here are a few tips for preparing them.

✦ To tell whether a bean is fully cooked, squeeze it. There should be no hard core at the center. Be aware that cooking the beans with an acidic ingredient, such as with tomatoes, will slow down their cooking time.

✦ If you're making beans as a side dish, add a small amount of brown sugar or molasses at the end of cooking for a delicious flavor.

✦ You can make dry beans less gassy by soaking them overnight with fennel seeds. Use a teaspoon of fennel per pound of beans.

Cooking Corn

Never add salt to the water when boiling corn; table salt contains traces of calcium, which will toughen the kernels. Instead, add a little milk to the cooking water, which will bring out the sweetness of the corn.

Easy Eggplant

Fried or roasted eggplant is delicious, but if you try preparing it as-is, it will normally come out terribly bitter. Luckily, removing this bitter taste is easy. Before preparing it, first cut it into thick slices. Salt the slices, and let them drain on a wire rack or in a colander for 30 minutes. Then rinse them well and pat dry. This procedure will also reduce the amount of oil they absorb during frying.

● Who Knew?

In a recent study, fried eggplant was found to absorb more fat than any other vegetable—even more than an equal portion of French fries.

Mushroom Maker

Mushrooms can be kept white and firm during sautéing if you add ¼ teaspoon lemon juice for every 2 tablespoons butter or olive oil.

Getting Rid of Celery Strings

For the most part, celery is easy to cook—the pectin in its cells breaks down easily in water. However, celery strings, which are made of cellulose, are virtually indestructible and won't break down at all under normal cooking conditions. Even the body has a difficult time breaking the strings down, and many people can't digest them at all. Be sure to remove the strings before preparing celery with this simple trick: Once you remove a stalk from the bunch, place it curved-side up on the counter or a cutting board, then grab hold of the very bottom (white part) of the stalk and quickly bend it up. It will crack off the bottom off the celery, but the strings will still be attached. Now all you need to do is simply pull this piece up toward the leaves, pulling as many strings with it as you can.

Cooking Brussels Sprouts

Brussels sprouts are an excellent source of vitamins A and C, and although they get a bad rap, our kids adore them. Store Brussels sprouts in the fridge to prevent their leaves from turning yellow. Cut an X on the stalk end of a Brussels sprout before cooking it, and it will cook evenly and quickly.

Perfect Peas

Here's a quick tip for one of our favorite vegetables: When cooking shelled, fresh peas, always add a few washed pods to the water. This will improve the flavor and give the peas a richer green color.

Sprightly Spinach

When cooking spinach, always do it in an uncovered pot. The steam that builds up when a pot is covered causes the plant's volatile acids to condense on the lid and fall back into the water. Keeping the lid off will make sure your spinach keeps its lovely green color.

Who Knew? Readers' Favorite

Baking stuffed apples, tomatoes, or bell peppers in a well-greased muffin tin will help them to hold their shape—and make sure they don't tip over when you take them out of the oven.

Cauliflower Cooking

Cauliflower cooks in 10–15 minutes, and overcooking will cause it to turn dark and tough, so make sure to keep an eye on the pot when boiling cauliflower. Add a small amount of lemon juice to the water to keep it white during cooking, and to reduce the odor of cooking cauliflower, replace the hot water when it's halfway through its cooking time. Never cook cauliflower in an aluminum or iron pot, because contact with these metals will turn cauliflower yellow, brown, or blue-green!

Beet Red

To make sure beets keep their red color through the entire cooking process, cook them whole with at least two inches of stem still attached, and add a few tablespoons of white vinegar to the water.

Vitamins and minerals are very important to your pet's health. Save the water from steamed or boiled vegetables or liquid from a slow cooker and mix it with your animal's food for additional nutrients—and a "human food" treat they'll love!

Your Dogs Will Thank Us

If you're cooking a chicken or turkey and don't have a use for the giblets, go ahead and cook them up for your dogs or cats. (You can usually just zap them in the microwave for a few minutes.) It's less pet food you'll have to buy and even more love you'll receive from your furry friend. Just make sure not to feed your pets too much "human food," as they may have trouble digesting it.

Never Pay for a Milk-Bone Again

When getting a "treat" for being good, most dogs are just excited about a special snack, not that it's in the shape of a bone. The truth is, doggie treats have almost the exact same ingredients as dog food, and most dogs can't tell the difference. Instead of paying extra for dog treats, keep a separate container of dog food where you normally keep the treats, then give your dog a small handful when he's done something reward-worthy. You'll save money on dog treats, but your dog will be just as happy.

CHAPTER 14

Desserts

Baker's Delight

Here's a neat tip for those who do a lot of baking. Fill a salt shaker with confectioners' or colored sugar for dusting candy, cakes, and cookies. Choose one with large holes for best results.

For the Sake of the Cake

If a cake recipe calls for flouring the baking pan, use some of the dry cake mix instead. The cake will absorb the mix, and you won't have a floury mess on the outside when the cake is done.

Who Knew? Readers' Favorite

To keep the frosting from sticking to your knife as you cut the cake, dip your knife into a glass of cold water between each cut.

Egg Substitution

When baking a cake, try substituting two egg yolks for one whole egg. The cake will be very rich and dense, because the yolks won't hold as much air as the whites. This isn't exactly a healthy tip, but it sure tastes good!

Keeping Your Cake Light

For a light, moist cake, enhance your cake flour by adding 2 tablespoons cornstarch to every cup of cake flour, then sifting them together before you add to the mix. You may be surprised by the results!

Popping Cake Bubbles

Make sure you get rid of any bubbles in your cake batter before baking it. This is easily accomplished by holding the pan an inch or two above the counter and tapping it two or three times to release any air pockets. Just be careful—the batter might spatter.

We Heart Cakes

A heart-shaped cake is easier to make than you might think. Simply divide your cake batter between one round pan and one square one. When the cakes are cool, cut the round cake in half. Turn the square cake so it looks like a diamond and set the half-rounds on the two top sides. Voilà!

Cool Cake Trick

If you're about to show off your cake prowess by cutting up baked cakes and re-assembling them in an impressing configuration, try freezing the cake first. Fresh cakes, especially those made from a mix, often crumble easily, but freezing will make your knife glide right through. Freezing detracts little from the taste of your cake, as long as you don't frost it first.

Cake Magic

If you find icing too sweet or too rich, try this cake topping: Set a paper lace doily on the cake, and then dust lightly with confectioners' sugar. Carefully lift the doily off the cake for a beautiful design left behind. Try colored confectioners' sugar or a mixture of confectioners' sugar and cocoa powder.

Here's a new twist on transporting frosted cakes. Don't just insert toothpicks and cover in plastic, because the sharp ends can puncture the plastic and result in a gooey mess. Instead, attach miniature marshmallows to the toothpicks before covering. Stands of spaghetti can also be used instead of toothpicks.

Keep a Cake from Sticking

Does your cake stick to the plate? Sprinkle a thin layer of sugar on a plate before you put a cake on it. This keeps the cake from sticking, and makes the bottom delightfully crunchy.

Stale Cake Cure

If you need to store a cake more than a day or two, put half an apple in the container. The apple will provide just enough moisture to keep the cake from drying out too soon.

Frost in Translation

Want to freeze a cake, but don't want the frosting to stick to the plastic wrap? Here's a handy tip for doing just that. First, put it in the freezer without any wrapping, Once the frosting is frozen, cover the cake with plastic wrap. The cold frosting won't stick to the wrap.

When your recipe calls for creaming butter or shortening with sugar, be sure you beat it for the entire time specified in the recipe. Shortening the time may yield a coarse-textured or heavy cake.

Awesome Icing Hints

Even if you've just made the most delicious cake ever, it still won't be a hit unless your finishing touch—the icing—holds its own. Here are a few of our favorite tips for perfect icing.

✦ If you sprinkle a very thin layer of cornstarch on top of a cake before you ice it, the icing won't run down the sides.

✦ To keep icing from hardening, just add a very small amount of white vinegar to the icing after it is whipped. You can also add a pinch of baking soda to the confectioners' sugar. This will help the icing retain some moisture and it will not dry out as fast.

✦ If you're making your own chocolate icing, add a teaspoon of unsalted butter to the chocolate while it is melting to improve the consistency.

✦ Here's a great bakers' trick to make it easier to decorate the top of a cake: With a toothpick, trace the pattern, picture, or lettering before you pipe the icing on. This will give you a guide, so you'll make fewer mistakes.

✦ If you're having a problem keeping a layer cake together when you're icing it, stick a few bamboo skewers into the cake through both layers; remove them as you're frosting the top.

Keep Leftover Cake Moist

If you have leftover cake, you have more self-control than we do! One of the best methods of keeping the insides of a cake from drying out is to place a piece of fresh white bread next to the exposed surface. The bread can be affixed with a toothpick or a short piece of spaghetti.

Three Cures for Domed Cakes

Unfortunately, part of baking is always trial and error. If your cakes "dome" when baked, it may be caused by one of these common errors: The oven temperature was too high, your pan was too small, or the balance of liquid, egg, flour, and fat was off. Time for a new trial!

● Who Knew?

The texture of a cake depends on the type of sweetener and fat used. These ingredients affect how tender the cake will be, so be sure you use the right ones. Never substitute granulated sugar for confectioners' sugar; granulated sugar is recommended for baking most cakes. Cakes made with oil are very tender and moist—oil doesn't hold air as well as butter or shortening, so eggs and other thick ingredients must trap the air.

Angel Food Aid

Never bake an angel food cake on the top or middle rack of the oven. It will retain moisture better if baked in the lower third of the oven, and always at the temperature specified in the recipe.

Angel Food Fact

An angel food cake can be left in the pan and covered tightly with foil for up to 24 hours or until you are ready to frost it.

Say Cheesecake!

When preparing a cheesecake, go exactly by the recipe and don't make any substitutions. You'll have a better chance at success if you follow the recipe to the letter. Here are some other pointers for perfect cheesecake.

+ Be sure that the cream cheese is at room temperature before using it.

+ When you bake a cheesecake at a lower temperature, there's less chance of it shrinking from the sides of the pan.

+ Never open the oven for the first 30 minutes when baking cheesecake! The cheesecake may develop cracks or partially collapse.

+ Cheesecakes will develop cracks when they are overcooked. They're done when the center of the cake is still wobbly and shaky—which may look underdone to you.

- Flourless cheesecakes need to be baked in a pan of water (called a water bath) to keep the eggs from coagulating.

- Cheesecake cracks can be repaired with whipped cream cheese or sweetened sour cream, but you'll be able to see the repair. It's better to top the cake with berries if it has too many cracks.

- Never substitute a different size pan for a cheesecake recipe—make sure to use the exact size recommended.

Keep Ice Off Your Ice Cream

It's always disappointing when you remember you have one last bit of ice cream in the freezer, only to open it and find it's covered in ice crystals. To keep this from happening, store your ice cream container in a sealed plastic bag in the freezer. It will stop ice crystals from forming. You can also cover the top of your ice cream with aluminum foil before you put the lid on top.

Who Knew? Readers' Favorite

Keep your ice cream cones leak-free with this simple tip: Place a miniature marshmallow or chocolate kiss in the bottom of the cone before adding the ice cream. Either of them can help prevent to tip of the cone from leaking—and are a delicious treat at the end of the cone!

Banana Fun

A great and healthy summer treat for kids is to cut a banana in half (horizontally, not vertically), put a popsicle stick in the flat end, dip it in some melted chocolate or sundae topping, and freeze it for a few hours on waxed paper. Your kids will love you for these banana treats! (At least for a little while.)

Shimmering Pies

Do you want your pies to glisten like those in the bakery? It's easy with this trick: Just beat an egg white and brush it over the crust before baking. This works especially well for a pie that has a crust cover, like apple pie.

Tips for a Flaky Crust

Even if your pie's filling is near perfection, you won't win any accolades for your creation unless its crust is up to par. Here are a few tips for making perfectly flaky pie crusts.

- ✦ Be sure the liquid going into your piecrust is ice cold. In fact, anything hot going into a pie crust will affect it. Be sure that even your kitchen and equipment are on the cool side.

- ✦ Add a teaspoon of vinegar to the water for an even flakier crust, or substitute sour cream or whipping cream for the entirety of the water.

- ✦ Low-gluten flour such as pastry flour is the best choice when you're making piecrusts. Cake flour is too soft and won't give the crust the body it needs, and bread flour contains too much gluten content to make a tender crust. As a substitute for pastry flour, combine 2 parts all-purpose flour and 1 part cake flour or instant flour.

✦ Replace the shortening or butter with lard. Lard has larger fat crystals and three times the polyunsaturates as butter, which will make the crust flakier.

Pie Dough Know-How

Never stretch pie dough when you are placing it in the pan. Stretched dough usually shrinks from the sides.

Prevent a Pie Crust Mess

Making graham cracker pie crust can turn into quite a mess—particularly when pressing the crumbs into the pie plate with greasy, buttered hands. Stop the crumbs from sticking by putting your hands into a plastic bag before the pressing begins!

Pie Serving Secret

Pies with graham cracker crusts can be difficult to remove from the pan. However, if you dip the bottom of the pan in warm water for 10 seconds, the pie will come right out without any damage.

Pumpkin Pie Loves Marshmallows

For a unique pumpkin pie, put small marshmallows on the bottom of the pie, just above the crust. As the pie bakes, the air in the marshmallows expands and the marshmallows rise to the top.

Most recipes tell you to be sure pie dough is chilled before putting it in the pie plate. Why? Cold will help to firm up the fat and relax the gluten in the flour. This helps it to retain its shape and reduce shrinkage.

Get Rid of Soggy Bottoms

It's always disappointing when you slice into your carefully prepared pie only to find that the bottom is soggy. If you have a problem with fruit or fruit juices soaking the bottom of your piecrust and making it too wet, brush the bottom crust with egg white before adding the filling. This will seal the piecrust and solve the problem. If your fruit filling is simply too wet, thicken it up. The best thickener is 3–4 tablespoons of minute tapioca. Just mix it with the sugar before adding to the fruit. Other solutions for soggy pie bottoms include prebaking the piecrust, partially cooking the filling, or brushing the crust with jelly before you fill it. When using a cream filling in a pie, sprinkle the crust with granulated sugar before adding the filling to eliminate a soggy crust.

Cutting a Creamy Pie

Spray a small amount of vegetable oil on your knife before cutting a pie with a cream filling. This will stop the filling from sticking to the knife.

For Extra Tasty Tarts

Here's a pastry chef's trick to add flavor to a lemon tart or pie: Rub a few sugar cubes over an orange or lemon, then include the cubes in the recipe as part of the total sugar. The sugar tends to extract just enough of the natural oils from the peels of the fruits to add some flavor.

Tender Pastries

Add some sugar to your pastry recipe to help tenderize the dough. Pastry dough should look like coarse crumbs after you cut in the fat (butter, shortening, etc.).

Fire up Your Flambé

If you're making a flambéed dish, you have more guts than us! Just be warned that you may have trouble igniting brandy when it's not hot enough. Some chefs warm the brandy gently before adding it to food to ensure that it will light. If you heat it too much before adding it to the dish, however, it may ignite too soon. Serving a dessert that's flambéed? Try soaking sugar cubes briefly in lemon or orange extract that contains alcohol, then set them on the dessert and carefully ignite.

A Lower-Cal Cookie

If you're making cookies, choose the soft drop, more-cakey versions rather than the rolled variety—they generally contain more air per serving and therefore, fewer calories.

Dough To-Do

When you mix cookie dough, only stir as much as you have to to fully combine the ingredients—overstirring can cause the cookies to become tough. Unbaked cookie dough may be frozen and unthawed when you're ready to make cookies. Wrap as airtight as possible in a freezer bag, try to resist not eating any, and stick in the freezer for up to one month.

Chilly Dough

Cold cookie dough will not stick to the rolling pin. Refrigerate the dough for 20 minutes for the best results.

Avoid Heavy Baked Goods

To keep cookies or butter cakes from becoming too heavy, be sure the butter is at room temperature before you cream it with the sugar. Try to avoid softening butter in the microwave, as it's easy to melt.

Who Knew?

Reduced-fat margarine, margarine spreads, and whipped butter should not be used for baking. They have too much water and air, which can cause cakes or cookies to collapse or flatten out. Always use the type of butter or margarine called for in the recipe.

Margarine Mayhem

When making cookies with margarine, the firmness of the dough will depend on the type of margarine used. Be sure to use stick margarine, not margarine from a tub. Be aware that margarine made from 100 percent corn oil will make the dough softer. When using margarine to make cookies, you may need lengthen the chilling time or place the dough in the freezer instead of the refrigerator. If you're making cutout cookies, the chilling time should be at least one hour in the refrigerator. Dough for drop and bar cookies doesn't have to be chilled.

Maintain the Moisture

Keep soft cookies, cakes, and pancakes deliciously moist by adding a teaspoon of jelly to the batter.

For Delicious Oatmeal Cookies

Our favorite part of oatmeal cookies, is—naturally—the oatmeal! When you make oatmeal cookies, boost the oatmeal's flavor by toasting it lightly before adding it to the batter. Simply sprinkle the oatmeal on a baking sheet and heat it in a 300° oven for about 10 minutes. The oats should turn a golden-brown.

● Who Knew?

If you are using 100 percent whole-wheat flour and want the crunchiest cookies ever, try using butter instead of another shortening. Never use oil, as it will make the cookies spread too fast when baked.

Burned Bottoms?

If you've ever burned the bottoms of your cookies when baking a number of batches, the baking sheets may be to blame. Let the baking sheets cool between batches—when you start with too hot a surface the cookies may burn. Two to three minutes cooling time is usually long enough. Another alternative is to line the baking sheets with parchment paper—simply lift the cookies, still on the parchment paper, onto the cooling rack.

Cookie Cooling

Cookies can go from just right to burned in no time. To lessen the chance of this happening, take the cookies out of the oven when they are not quite done, but don't transfer them to the cooling rack right away—let them sit on the hot pan for a minute or two to finish baking. Once you transfer them to the rack, be sure to let them fully cool before you store them; otherwise, they risk becoming soggy.

Browning Cookies

If your cookies typically don't brown enough, bake them on a higher rack in the oven. Other techniques to boost the browning of cookies are substituting a tablespoon or two of corn syrup for the sugar, using egg for the liquid, and using unbleached or bread flour in the recipe.

Cookie Dough Spoon Saver

Is your cookie dough sticking to everything? It's easy to get a spoonful of cookie dough to drop to your baking pan if you first dip the spoon in milk.

Cookie Cutter Tip

To get a sharp edge on your cookies when using cutters, dip the cutter in flour or warm oil occasionally during the cutting.

Crisper Cookies

If crisp cookies are what you're after, be sure your cookie jar has a loose-fitting lid. This allows air to circulate and evaporates any moisture.

To keep your cookies tasting chewy, add a half an apple or a slice of white bread to the cookie jar. This will provide just enough moisture to keep the cookies from becoming hard.

Storing Cookies

Rinse out coffee cans and store cookies in them. Use the original lids, or stretch plastic wrap across the top and seal with a rubber band.

Getting Your Brownies Out of a Sticky Situation

If your baked foods are stuck to the bottom of the pan, wrap the bottom of the pan in a cold, wet towel for a few minutes. Once the pan is cooler, your brownies or bar cookies may come out much more easily.

Whip It Good

Whipping up some cream? Heavy cream will set up faster if you add seven drops of lemon juice for each pint of cream. But you don't necessarily need heavy cream if you're making whipped cream. Light cream can be whipped to a firm, mousse-like consistency if you add 1 tablespoon unflavored gelatin that has been dissolved in 1 tablespoon hot water for every 2 cups of cream. After whipping, refrigerate it for two hours.

How to Get the Creamiest Custard

Making perfect custard takes time and patience, but these tips should help. For a super-rich custard, add 2–3 egg yolks in addition to your usual amount of eggs. For a custard that is creamy rather than solid, stir the mixture continuously over low heat to keep the protein from setting too quickly. The milk helps separate the egg proteins from one another, which allows the custard to coagulate at a higher temperature and reduces the possibility of curdling. So never replace the milk with water, because your custard will not set. You should also never try to speed up the cooking process by increasing the heat.

Meringue Magic

Not only is homemade meringue delicious, it will also impress your friends…especially if you use these tips for getting the best meringue and the highest peaks.

✦ Make sure that your egg whites are at room temperature. As you beat, add 2–3 tablespoons of superfine or granulated sugar for each egg used. Keep beating until the peaks stand up without drooping.

✦ For the fluffiest egg whites, add a pinch of salt before whipping, and use a copper bowl if you happen to have one.

✦ To keep the peaks firmer for a longer period of time, add ⅛ teaspoon of white vinegar per egg white while beating. To get more meringue per egg white, add 2 teaspoons cold water for each egg white before beating.

✦ How do you know if beaten egg whites are stiff enough? Just run a knife through the middle of the bowl—if the whites stay separated, they're ready.

◆ Remember, if it's rainy (or even damp) outside, the meringue peaks will not remain upright! It might be better to save your baking for a drier day.

◆ Occasionally, meringue will develop small droplets of water on its surface shortly after it is removed from the oven. This beading is caused by overcooking, so to prevent this, bake meringue at a high temperature (between 400° and 425°) for a short time—4 to 5 minutes.

Syrup Secrets

When boiling syrup, one of the more frequent and annoying problems is that it crystallizes. The easiest way to avoid this is to put a pinch of cream of tartar in the syrup while it's cooking. This adds a small amount of acidity—just enough to prevent crystals from forming but not enough that you should taste it.

Making Candy?

Cooking up your own candy is as delicious as it is fun. Experienced candy makers know that keeping the sugar from crystallizing during cooking is a big problem. There's a simple solution: Heat the sugar over low heat, without stirring, until it's completely dissolved. To dissolve any sugar crystals that cling to the sides of the pan, cover the pan with a tight-fitting lid and continue cooking the syrup for three to four minutes. The steam that's generated will melt these pesky sugar crystals.

The Collapsible Soufflé

Be careful when you're making a soufflé. Air bubbles are trapped when you beat the egg whites, and when a soufflé is placed in the oven, the air expands, causing the soufflé to rise. If the soufflé is punctured or shaken, the air will be released too early and the soufflé will collapse. It's also true that a soufflé must be served as soon as it is removed from the oven. Soufflés begin to collapse as soon as they start to cool down. So it's best to serve them in the baking dish.

The Perfect Coffee-Topper

To make milk "foam" for the top of your coffee or cappuccino, fill a small saucepan halfway with cold milk. While heating on medium-high, slowly beat the milk with a loose wire whisk. As the milk heats up, beat more quickly—the bubbles should become smaller and be closer together. When the milk is hot, remove from the heat and continue to whisk until the foam has doubled in size. Just make sure the milk doesn't boil, or it will curdle and you'll have to start over!

Sweet 'n' Easy Coffee

If you love flavored coffee with your dessert and take yours with sugar, simply mix ¼ teaspoon fresh vanilla bean or 1 teaspoon cinnamon with 1 cup of sugar in a food processor for 1 minute, then keep next to your sugar for a delicious-tasting sweetener! It's usually much cheaper than buying flavored coffees or creamers, and tastes better, too.

CHAPTER 15

Parties and Special Occasions

Hot Cross Buns

Having a dinner party? Here's a great tip for keeping dinner rolls warm long after they've come out of the oven. When you put the rolls in the oven to bake, put a ceramic tile in, too. By the time the rolls are done, the tile will be (very!) hot. Place it in the basket and put your rolls on top. The tile will keep them warm. You can also use aluminum foil instead of the tile, but it won't retain the heat as long.

For Cheese Plate Praises

Always bring cheese to room temperature one hour before serving it. Even if the cheese becomes a little melty, the flavor will be much better.

Who Knew? Readers' Favorite

To keep meat or cheese hors d'oeuvres moist, cover them with a damp paper towel, then cover loosely with plastic wrap. Many fillings (as well as bread) dry out very quickly, but with this tip, you can make these simple appetizers first and have them ready on the table when guests arrive.

Creative Fruit Display

For a fun display on your buffet table, hollow out a melon, orange, or grapefruit and fill it with cut-up fruits (and maybe even some miniature marshmallows). For a more attractive holder, you can scallop the edges or cut it in the shape of a basket.

Is That My Wine?

Having a party? Instead of buying "wine rings," which go around the base of wine glasses to mark whose drink is whose, simply have a dry-erase marker on-hand and have guests write their names (or a funny message) right on their glass.

Saving Wine

Wondering what to do with leftover wine (besides drinking it, of course)? Keep it fresh by putting whatever is left in a small container such as a jam jar. This limits the amount of air the wine is put in contact with, keeping it fresh. Incidentally, that is the same thing those expensive "wine vacuum sealers" do!

● Who Knew?

In the United States, white wine is much more popular than red wine. The top-consumed wine is chardonnay, followed by white zinfandel.

A "Cool" Idea

To keep ice cubes from melting at a party, put them in a bowl, and then set that bowl in a larger one filled with dry ice.

Keep Your Punch Cold

Drinking punch that's half water is never fun, but ice cubes can melt so quickly when left out in a bowl. One of the easiest ways to keep a large punch bowl cold is to make larger ice cubes, as it will take one giant ice cube much longer to melt than many little ones. To make a long-lasting, large cube, fill a rinsed-out milk or juice carton half-full with water. Then peel off the cardboard when it's time to use.

Ice Cube Math

If you run out of ice at a party, you're in trouble! But how do you know how much to buy? Use this simple metric. If you're serving mostly cocktails, the average person at a party will go through 10–15 cubes. When you buy ice cubes in the bag, you will get about 10 cubes per pound.

Party Time!

Here's a cute way of sending out unique party invitations. Write the invite on a blown-up balloon with a permanent marker, then deflate it and put them in the mail. Your guests will have to blow up the balloon to read the invitation.

Eliminate the Drip

Don't spend extra for dripless candles—you can make "regular" candles dripless with this simple procedure. Place the candles in a shallow pan and add enough water to cover them. Then add 2 tablespoons salt per candle, and mix or agitate until the salt dissolves (you might want to take the candles out while mixing, then put them back in). Let the candles soak in the saltwater for two to three hours, then rinse them and let them dry. Wait at least 24 hours before you use the candles, and they'll be virtually dripless. The salt water hardens the wax, which makes it burn more slowly and cleanly, reducing the chance of drips onto linens or furniture.

A Must for Candles

Bringing out the candles for your party? Put them in the freezer the night before, and they'll burn more slowly and drip less when you take them out.

Who Knew? Readers' Favorite

You just had a great dinner party, except now there's wax all over your candlesticks. To remove candle wax from just about anything, simply put it in the freezer. Leave for a couple of hours and the wax will peel off easily.

Marshmallow Candleholders

To add a little color and whimsy to a birthday cake, make natural candleholders from small marshmallows, which will protect your cake from melting wax. Keep them refrigerated for best results. The best part is that you can give them to guests to eat after the candles are burned out, as long as they don't have any wax on them.

A Thoughtful and Thrifty Gift for a Bride-to-Be

Here's a wonderful, one-of-a-kind gift for a bridal shower: Buy a blank hardcover book, add dividers, and create a family cookbook. Just ask the bride and groom's families to provide their favorite treasured recipes.

Sending Flowers?

If you're sending flowers for a special occasion, skip the national delivery services and websites. Instead, find a flower shop that is local to the recipient and call them directly. Most national services simply charge you a fee, then contact these very same stores themselves.

DIY Easter Egg Dye

It's easy to make natural Easter egg dyes. Just add colorful ingredients to the water while you boil your eggs. Use grass for green, onionskins for yellow and deep orange, and beets for pink. If you plan to eat the eggs, be sure to use plants that haven't been fertilized or treated with pesticides or other chemicals.

Halloween Pumpkin Preserver

A problem we used to have every Halloween was that our pumpkins got soft and mushy soon after they were carved. It turns out that this happens because air comes in contact with the inside flesh, allowing bacteria to grow. So to solve the problem of every jack-o-lantern looking like an old man, we now spray the inside of the hollowed-out pumpkin with an antiseptic spray, which slows down the bacterial growth and increases the time it takes for the pumpkin to deteriorate. Just make sure no one eats a pumpkin that has been sprayed!

Save on Your Tree Skirt

Don't waste your money on an expensive tree skirt this Christmas. Instead, look for a small, round table cloth from a department store—they usually have a big selection and they're inexpensive, too. Cut a round opening in the center for the tree stand, and a straight line to one edge. Place the opening in the back of the tree and you're done.

Long Live Christmas

We've been known to keep our Christmas tree up until well into January, and with this little trick, you can enjoy the holidays a little longer too. Add a small amount of sugar or Pine-Sol to the water to extend the life of your tree.

The Windup on Christmas Lights

When you take down your Christmas tree, always wrap the lights around the outside of a cardboard tube (try the tube from a roll of paper towels) and secure with masking tape. They'll be easy to unwind next year, and you'll never have another nightmarish day of untangling all the lights while the kids wait to decorate the tree.

Safe Storage for Holiday Decorations

When it's time to bring down the tree and lights, take great care with the more delicate ornaments. Slip them into old socks or nylons; for extra safety, then place them in disposable plastic cups before storing. Old egg cartons are another ultra-safe (and eco-friendly) way to store bulbs and glass trinkets.

CHAPTER 16

The Perfect Barbecue

Get Your Grill In Shape for BBQ Season

When Memorial Day rolls around, make sure your outdoor grill is prepped for the first barbecue of the season. Clean the grates by placing them in the tub and covering with very hot water and one cup each ammonia and dishwasher detergent. Cover with old fabric softener sheets and soak overnight. The next day, don your rubber gloves, scrub away, and watch the grease dissolve.

Today's News: A Clean Grill!

A great way to clean your barbecue grill is with wet newspaper. After cooking, just place it on a warm grill for one hour with the lid closed. You'll be amazed how easily the grime comes off!

Great Grilling

Spraying your grill with a bit of vegetable oil before you start grilling will make cleaning ever easier, and your grill even hotter (which will put those cool "grill marks" on your meat and veggies). For the easiest clean-up, coat the grill with vegetable (or canola) oil before starting the fire, then wipe it with a wet rag shortly after you are through. Never spray the oil on the grill after the fire has started—it may cause a flare-up.

Who Knew?

The United States consumes more hot dogs than the rest of the world combined—28 million in ballparks alone last year.

A Tasty Grill

To help reduce smoke and improve the flavor of food on your grill, use an onion! Cut a red onion in half, pierce it with a fork, and dip in water. Then use the onion half to wipe down the grill rack.

Tongs Are Terrific

Always use tongs when turning meat on the grill. When a fork pierces the meat, it releases some of its juices, making it dry out more quickly.

Keep Chicken from Stickin'

When grilling chicken, always grease the rack well. Why? Because as the bird cooks, the collagen in the skin turns into a sticky gelatin, which will cause it to stick to the rack. Another way to solve the problem is to sear the chicken on the grill, and then finish it in a preheated oven 15 to 20 minutes, breast-side up.

Prevent a Barbecue Blunder

Remember that barbecue sauces contain sugar, and high heat can burn the sugar as well as some of the spices in the sauce. Never apply the sauce until about five minutes before your meat is fully cooked. Another secret is to use low heat and leave the meat on the grill for a longer period.

The Hubbub About Rubs

Applying a rub is a common method of seasoning the surface of meats and poultry. A rub is simply a blend of various herbs and spices that doesn't penetrate the meat. The rub never blends with the flavor of the meat itself, but it does provide a tasty coating, which usually forms a brown crust of concentrated flavor. (Yum!) Rub on the seasoning before you begin to grill the meat, and let it sit awhile for the coating to take hold.

Burger Buzzkill

While undercooked burgers may pose a risk of *E. coli* poisoning, well-done burgers may pose the risk of a potentially harmful carcinogen called heterocyclic aromatic amine (HAA). This compound is formed when meat is cooked at too high a temperature. To avoid HAA, try these tips:

✦ Choose lean cuts of beef. Ask the butcher to remove all the fat from around the edges and put it through the meat grinder twice to break up the remaining fat. Sizzling fat creates smoke, which creates HAA.

✦ Place the ground beef in a microwave oven on high power for 1 to 3 minutes just before you cook it. HAAs form when browning occurs, but precooking meat before it goes onto the grill reduces the amount of time HAAs have to form.

✦ Reduce the amount of meat in your burgers by adding mashed black beans, cottage cheese, or cooked rice and you will have a safer—not to mention delicious—medium-well burger.

For a Juicy Steak

Some backyard cooks think that searing a steak at a high temperature will keep the juices in. Nonsense! Searing does cause the browning that creates a good flavor, but it doesn't seal in the juices. A steak cooked slowly and at a lower temperature is more tender and retains more of its juices. If you want to sear a steak, only do it for a minute or two on each side, then lower the temperature and let it cook more slowly.

Speedier Grilling

When you are grilling for a crowd and your grill isn't big enough, you can save time by utilizing your oven, too. Place a few layers of hamburgers between sheets of foil on a cookie sheet and bake them in a 350° oven for 15 minutes. Then throw them on the grill for 5–10 minutes more, and they'll be fully cooked but still have that grilled taste. Hot dogs may be done the same way, but only bake them for 10 minutes.

Thick Is the Trick for Grilling Fish

If you plan on grilling fish, be sure to purchase steaks that are at least 1-inch thick. Fish dries out very quickly on the grill, so the thicker it is the better. The skin should be left on fillets while grilling and removed after they are cooked.

Lemon Aid

Grilling fish is always a drag because the skin inevitably gets stuck to the grate—particularly when cooking salmon. Avoid this by placing a few thin slices on lemon or lime on the grill, and then the fish on top.

Not only will your clean-up be easier, but the citrus flavor will taste great with the seafood.

The Best Way to Skewer Shrimp

When grilling shrimp, always thread the them onto the skewers lengthwise, so they won't curl on the grill. They'll also be less likely to fall into the fire.

Perfect Grilled Corn

Doing some grilling? Impress your guests by barbecuing fresh corn to perfection this way: Before grilling, peel all but the innermost layer of husk from the corn, and trim the excess silks as well. Place on the grill and as soon as the husk darkens enough that the outline of the kernels are visible through it, remove the corn. It will be perfectly cooked and have a wonderful, smoky flavor.

Who Knew?

Corn is one vegetable that is always better eaten when it is fresh, preferably on the day it was picked. As soon as corn is picked, its sugars start to convert to starch. The milky liquid in the kernel that makes corn sweet will turn pulpy and bland in as little as two to three days. If you've only eaten corn from a supermarket, stop at a farm stand one day and pick up some ears that have just been picked. You're sure to marvel at the difference in flavor and texture.

Veggies on the Grill

When grilling vegetables in aluminum foil on the grill, try placing a sprig of a fresh herbs within each foil wrap. Marjoram is the most popular choice, but almost any herb will do: Try tarragon, Italian parsley, sage, chives, dill, chervil, oregano, and thyme. It will give your veggies a fresh, wonderful taste.

Potato Salad Trick

If you would like a richer color to your potato salad (and who doesn't), try adding a small amount of mustard when you are mixing it.

For Divine Deviled Eggs

To keep yolks centered when boiling eggs for deviled eggs, stir the water while they are cooking. To keep them from wobbling on the platter when they're done, cut a thin slice off two sides of the egg before you halve it lengthwise. This will give each egg half a flat base.

The Coal Truth

Though they may be more work than a gas grill, charcoal grills impart an amazing smoky flavor into meats and veggies. Here are a few tips to get the most out of your charcoal grill.

- ✦ To add flavor to barbecued foods, place dried herbs on the hot coals. Some of our favorites are savory, rosemary, and basil.

- ✦ If the coals become too hot or flare up, squirt them with water from a mister or a bulb baster.

✦ Store charcoal briquettes in airtight plastic bags—they absorb moisture very easily and won't be as easy to light if exposed to air.

Just Say No to More Lighter Fluid

When the coals start to die down on your grill, don't squirt them with more lighter fluid, which not only costs money, but can leave your food tasting bad (not to mention, burn the hair off your arm). Instead, blow a hair dryer on the base of the coals. The hairdryer acts as a pair of bellows, and your fire will be going again in no time.

How Much Coal?

When using a cookbook to make grilled foods, the recipe will often call for a certain amount of charcoal (for example, 5 quarts). To always know how much coal you're using, keep an old, washed-out milk carton with your charcoal stash. Open the top of the carton and it not only makes a great scoop, but you'll know you're getting 2 quarts of coal each time.

Another Grill-Cleaning Trick

Save on expensive grill cleaners by simply using WD-40 instead. Get rid of charred food stuck to the grill by removing it from the barbecue and spraying it with the oil. Let sit for 5–10 minutes, then wipe off and clean with soap and water.

To keep your cooler fresh and odor free, throw in 10–15 charcoal briquettes, close the top, and leave it overnight. In the morning, clean the cooler with soapy water, and it will smell like new.

For the Fastest Cold Beer

The best way to chill beer or soda rapidly is to fill a cooler with layers of water, ice, and salt, then plunge the beers inside. In about 20 minutes or less, the beer will be ice cold! Even if the ice water is warmer than your freezer, it absorbs the warmth from the bottles or cans more rapidly and more efficiently than the cold air of the freezer does. Just remember that premium lagers should be served between 42°F and 48°F and ales between 44°F and 52°F, so don't let them get too cold.

Frozen Grapes

If you want to keep your wine (or other beverage) cool on hot summer days, use frozen grapes instead of ice cubes. They'll keep the drink cold and they won't dilute it or change the taste as they thaw. Just make sure you wash them before freezing!

Perk Up Your Tabletops

Linoleum or vinyl floor tiles are excellent for covering picnic tabletops. You can also use linoleum on kitchen shelves, instead of contact paper. It will last longer and is easier to keep clean.

CHAPTER 17

Baking Tips

Flour Test

Not sure whether the flour in the canister is self-rising or all-purpose? Taste it. Self-rising flour will taste a bit salty because it contains baking powder.

Warm for Cakes, Cold for Pastries

When baking cakes and cookies, the ingredients should always be warm, never cold, to start. For pastry it is just the opposite—the ingredients should be cold.

The Need to Knead

Electric stand mixers are a boon for bakers, because the dough hook attachment reduces or eliminates the need to knead. To keep the dough from climbing up the hook, spray the hook with nonstick cooking spray or vegetable oil before turning the mixer on. This is also a great tip for when you're using a hand mixer.

Who Knew?

Although it may be tempting for health reasons, never omit the salt from your bread recipe. Salt strengthens and tightens the gluten, keeping bread from becoming crumbly.

Freezy Does It

Did you know you can freeze bread dough for later use? Let it rise once then punch it down, wrap well, and freeze. Don't forget to label it!

Moldy Bread?

You may know that you can usually just cut mold off of cheese, but the same does not hold true for bread. If you see the slightest sign of mold on baked goods, throw the item out. Mold often sends out "feelers" that can't be seen in most instances.

Yeast Saver

Where should you store yeast, you ask? Always in the refrigerator, because the cold will slow down deterioration. Bring the yeast back up to room temperature to help it dissolve at the normal rate.

Weak Flour?

Adding a bit of ascorbic acid (vitamin C) to flour when baking bread can help to strengthen weak flour. For every 6 cups flour, add a pinch of powdered ascorbic acid to the yeast. Ascorbic acid is easiest to find in the form of vitamin C tablets in the vitamin or cold remedy section of your drugstore.

Who Knew? Readers' Favorite

Consider keeping a clean powder puff in your flour container. It's a great way to dust flour onto rolling pins or pastry boards. And remember, always store your flour in the freezer to prevent any sort of bug infestation.

Perfectly Greased and Floured Pans

Recipes for baked goods often call for greased and floured pans, which usually involves oiling it down, then sprinkling flour inside and shaking the pan until it's equally distributed. However, professional bakers don't often use this method, which can leave flour on your baked goods or make them cook unevenly. Instead, they mix up a batch of "baker's magic," and now you can, too. Mix ½ cup room temperature vegetable shortening, ½ cup vegetable oil, and ½ cup all-purpose flour. Blend the mixture well and use it to grease pans. It can be stored in an airtight container in the refrigerator for up to six months.

Bread Pan Pandering

It's never good to be dull...unless you're a bread pan. For the best results when baking, never use a shiny bread pan. A shiny pan reflects heat to such a degree that the bread may not bake evenly. However, a dark pan may cook the bread too quickly, resulting in burned bottoms. Your best bet? A dull aluminum pan.

● Who Knew?

On humid or very hot days, yeast dough can rise faster than you expect and can become very hard to knead. When this occurs, there is a loss of elasticity, so you may want to save your baking day for one that is cooler.

Don't Overfill

Remember, never fill a baking pan more than half to two-thirds full. Cakes, muffins, and other baked goods need room to expand.

Muffin Tin Tip

Making cupcakes or muffins and don't have enough batter to fill the tin? Before sticking them in the oven, fill the empty holes in the tin halfway with water. It will extend the life of the tin and make sure the muffins bake evenly.

Blending Basics

When baking, it is important that all the ingredients be blended well, without being blended too much. If you need to sift flour, add the other dry ingredients (such as leavening and salt) to the flour before you sift.

Kneading Know-How

Don't skimp when kneading bread—it's what distributes the yeast and other ingredients evenly throughout the dough. If dough isn't kneaded properly, it won't rise evenly. Electric bread machines, stand mixers, and food processors have short work of this important task, but if you're kneading dough by hand, rub a small amount of vegetable oil onto your hands before you begin, which will make kneading thick dough easier. A wooden cutting board is your best bet for kneading bread, but other surfaces will work. Just be sure to flour the board adequately.

Who Knew?

After you've removed bread from the oven, always cool it on a wire rack. This will allow air to circulate around the bread and should eliminate any soggy areas in the loaf.

Dough Won't Rise?

One of the most frequent problems bread bakers encounter is yeast dough that doesn't rise adequately. If your dough won't rise, check out the following tips to see if you can pinpoint the reason your yeast isn't doing what you want it to.

✦ Your dough may be too cool, which reduces the level of yeast activity. Dough can rise at lower temperatures—even in the refrigerator—but it takes several hours or overnight to attain the same volume that it can in an hour or two at 80–90° F.

✦ The yeast may have been prepared with water that was too hot, which can kill it. The water must be under 120°F for optimum results.

✦ The yeast may have been too old. Proof the yeast before using it to be sure it's not ready for retirement. To proof yeast, dissolve a little sugar in some warm water, then sprinkle in the yeast. The mixture should begin bubbling within 5–7 minutes. If it doesn't, the yeast is too inactive to provide the leavening function, and should be thrown away.

The Secret to a Crispy Crust

We love this secret to a perfect loaf of bread, given to us by a baker friend: Put some ice cubes in a shallow pan and put in the oven with your loaf of bread. This will produce a dense steam, and as the water evaporates, the crust becomes hard and crispy. The steam also will allow the bread to rise more evenly, giving you a nice inside that's firm and chewy.

(Not Too Much) Garlic Bread

Want a hint of garlic without a too-garlicky taste? You can make a lightly scented garlic bread by adding 1 teaspoon of garlic powder to the flour when you're making white bread.

Flavored Crusts

Next time you make a pie, add a little flavor to the crust by adding a little ground spice or minced herbs to the flour. Use cinnamon or ginger with an apple or other dessert pie, and try finely chopped parsley with a quiche or meat pie.

Buttermilk: Not Always Bad for You

Buttermilk can be substituted for 2 percent or whole milk in most pastry or bread recipes. Buttermilk is less than 1 percent fat, almost equal to skim milk, but it has a thicker consistency.

Creamy Cream Cheese

When baking and your recipe calls for cream cheese, be sure it's at room temperature before you start, and make sure you beat it so it's light and fluffy before adding any other ingredients, especially eggs.

Flour the Fruit

Bread, muffins, and other baked goods are fun (and delicious) to make with dried fruits, but they often sink to the bottom because they lose some moisture and become more solid during baking. If you coat them with a little flour, though, they'll stay put.

Whole-wheat bread dough will not rise as high as bread dough made from all-purpose or bread flour. Whole-wheat flour is denser because it's not as refined. This is why most whole-wheat bread recipes blend whole-wheat flour with either bread flour or all-purpose flour.

Go Gently

If you make bread with 100 percent whole-wheat flour, it will be moister if you add the flour to the water slowly and mix gently. Whole-wheat flour absorbs water at a slower rate than do other types of flour. Reserve ¼ cup of flour and knead in a tablespoon or so at a time as needed.

What Kind of Crust Do You Want?

Using different liquids when making bread dough will impart different characteristics to the crust of your bread. Water, a common choice, will cause the top of the bread to be crisp, and it significantly intensifies the flavor of the wheat. Save some of the water you've used to boil potatoes and it will add a unique flavor to your bread, makes the crust smooth, and cause the dough to rise faster due to the high starch content. Milk gives bread a rich, creamy color and leaves the bread with a fine texture and a soft, brown crust. Eggs will provide a moister crust.

A liquid sweetener such as molasses, maple syrup, or honey will cause the crust to be dark brown and will also keep it moist. Vegetable or meat broth will give the bread a special flavor and provide you with a light, crisp crust. Alcohol of any type will give the bread a smooth crust with a flavor that may be similar to the alcohol used, especially beer; just don't use too much or you'll kill the yeast. Coffee and tea are commonly used to provide a dark, rich color and a crisp crust.

For Perfect Popovers

If you want the lightest popovers every time, puncture them with a fork when you remove them from the oven to release the air inside.

Puff Pastry Perfection

Puff pastry dough is made from flour, butter, and water. A small amount of butter is layered between dough that is folded several times to form as many as 700 layers. When you cut puff pastry dough, be sure to use a very sharp knife and cut straight down; never pull the knife through the dough or cut the dough at an angle. Doing so will cause the ends to puff up unevenly as the pastry bakes.

Removing Muffins

To easily remove muffins or rolls from a pan, set the pan on a damp towel for about 30 seconds. Use an old towel, because the pan might stick.

Beautiful Biscuits

Who doesn't love a tasty biscuit? Not only are they delicious, homemade biscuits are a great way to spruce up a leftover or frozen meal. Here are some tips and tricks for making the best-tasting biscuits.

✦ One secret to light biscuits: Handle the dough gently. Overworking the dough and re-rolling the scraps makes for tough biscuits.

✦ If your biscuits are heavy and dense, check your baking powder for freshness and make sure that you are properly sifting all the dry ingredients together. Even blending of the ingredients is key, so if you don't have a sifter, put the dry ingredients into a large sieve and shake them into the mixing bowl, or whisk them together.

✦ If you like your biscuits to be a rich golden color, add a teaspoon of sugar to the dry ingredients. It helps the crust to caramelize (and it only adds 16 calories to the whole batch!).

✦ If you're using a cutter to cut your biscuits, dip it in flour first so the dough won't stick to it. Be sure to press the cutter straight down—don't twist it even slightly. Doing so seals the edges of the biscuits and they won't rise as high.

✦ Shortening is the preferred fat for biscuits. Butter makes for a more solid biscuit, and oil makes them greasy.

✦ For super-soft biscuits, brush them with milk or melted
   unsalted butter before baking, then arrange them in a
   cake pan so the sides touch one another.

Glazing Over

Before you put rolls in the oven, make a delicious glaze for their tops
that your guests are sure to appreciate. Lightly beat an egg white with
a tablespoon of milk and brush on each roll. You'll love it!

Reheating Rolls

The quickest way to reheat biscuits or rolls? Sprinkle them lightly
with water and wrap them in foil. It should take about 5 minutes in a
preheated 350° oven.

Best Croutons Ever

If you really want to impress your dinner guests, make some
homemade croutons for your salad. Here's how: After cutting your
leftover bread into cubes, fry in olive oil and a little garlic powder (not
garlic salt), a pinch of parmesan cheese, and parsley. Fry until they're
brown, then let cool on paper towels. They freeze well, too!

Making the Cut

After making breads that don't require yeast—like pumpkin, zucchini,
and banana bread, as well as cornbread and scones—wait a day to
slice them (if you have the time). Waiting 24 hours before making an
incision will make your cuts less jagged and produce fewer crumbs.
For other types of bread, you only need to wait 15 minutes before
slicing.

How does baking powder work, you ask? Well, baking powder is a mixture of acids and alkalis that produce carbon dioxide when they come into contact with water and are subjected to certain temperatures. This carbon dioxide gas creates minute air pockets (or enters air pockets that already exist in the dough), as well as steam, which causes bread to expand.

Dough Cleaning Done Easily

When you're done with an afternoon of baking, sprinkle your messy countertop with salt, and the doughy, floury mess that you've left behind can be easily wiped away with a damp sponge.

Save Those Bread Bags

Don't forget to save your store-bought bread bags for times when you bake bread. They are perfectly sized bag for homemade breads.

For the Best Baked Sale Item

For your next bake sale, write out the recipe for your baked good on an index card and tape it to the plate or box that it came on. That way, if buyers find your goody to their liking, they'll know they can make it themselves in the future. They may also be more likely to buy your baked good if it comes with a free recipe!

CHAPTER 18

Making Your Food Last Longer

The Best Ways to Freeze Food

Freezing food is vital for being able to save money, because it allows you to buy food when it's on sale and make it when you have time, then save it for later. It seems like it should be as easy as just shoving food in the freezer, but there are a number of tips that will make your food taste better after defrosting.

✦ Never use quick-cooking rice in a dish that will be frozen, as it becomes mushy when reheated. Use regular or long-grain rice instead.

✦ Don't add toppings to dishes to be frozen; add when serving.

✦ When preparing most vegetables for freezing, they should be blanched, not fully cooked. This will lessen the enzymatic activity in the vegetable, and reheating will complete the cooking. To blanch, simply steam or boil for about half the time you normally would to cook them, then plunge the vegetables into ice water and drain. Potatoes and squashes are the exception to this rule—they should be fully cooked.

✦ Freezing causes russet or Idaho potatoes to fall apart; if you need them to stay whole or in chunks use potatoes with red skin or waxy flesh.

✦ Freezing tends to intensify the flavors of certain foods, such as garlic, peppers, and cloves. Use less in a dish that you will freeze, and when reheating, taste and add more as needed.

✦ On the other hand, use more onion than you would otherwise, because freezing tends to cause onion to lose its flavor. Herbs and salt also tend to diminish in flavor, so it's best to add them after freezing, when you're reheating the dish.

✦ Avoid freezing sauces. Egg-based sauces and those high in fat tend to separate when reheated, and cheese- or milk-based sauces are prone to curdling. Don't try to freeze mayonnaise, salad dressing, or jam. Most gravies will thicken considerably when frozen, but they can be thinned when reheated.

✦ Artificial sweeteners do not freeze well, so don't substitute them for sugar.

✦ Don't freeze any bakery item with a cream filling because it will become soggy. Custard and meringue pies, for example, don't freeze well. The custard tends to separate and the meringue becomes tough.

✦ Cool already-cooked foods in the refrigerator before freezing. Cooling them quickly prevents bacterial growth.

Prepare to be Frozen!

When you freeze foods, evaporation continues and fluids are lost. The entire surface of the meat must be protected from this process with a moisture-resistant wrap. The best way to wrap meats for freezing is in plastic wrap covered by a protective freezer paper or aluminum foil. This will not eliminate evaporation entirely, but it will reduce the risk of oxidation and rancidity.

How Long Does Raw Meat Keep in the Freezer?

Buying meat when it's on sale and keeping it in your freezer is a great way to save on groceries. Unfortunately, you can't keep it in there forever! Here is a helpful guide to how long different kinds (and cuts) of raw meat will keep at 0° F, the optimal temperature for your freezer.

Meat	Months
Bacon	1
Beef	9
Chicken (in parts)	9
Chicken (whole)	12
Cold cuts	1
Duck	4–6
Fish (fatty)	3
Fish (lean)	6
Goose	4–6
Ground beef	2–3
Ground pork	2–3
Ham	3
Pork (chops or ribs)	6–9
Pork roast	9
Rabbit	6–9
Sausage	2
Shellfish	4–6
Turkey (in parts)	6
Turkey (whole)	12
Venison	6–12

Consume It or Freeze It!

Small cuts of meat will spoil more quickly than larger cuts and should not be kept in the refrigerator for more than a day or two. Liver, sweetbreads, and cubed meats should be cooked within one day, or should be kept frozen.

Meatless Mondays

Never buy meat from the supermarket on Monday morning. It's likely that those for sale were not sold on the weekend, and most shipments of fresh meat arrive on Monday afternoon or on Tuesday.

Don't Always Ditch the Fat

It might sound counterintuitive, but buying fattier meat can actually help your food go further—and help your waistline stay intact. You're likely to eat less, assuming you cut off the fat when it's on your plate. And fattier meat generally has a better taste, so a little goes a longer way.

Who Knew? Readers' Favorite

To avoid the absorption of refrigerator odors, always store eggs in their original carton on an inside shelf of the refrigerator. Before you put away the carton, though, turn each egg upside down. Storing eggs with the tapered end down to maximizes the distance between the yolk and the air pocket, which may contain bacteria. The yolk is more perishable than the white, and even though it is more or less centered in the egg, the yolk can shift slightly and will move away from possible contamination.

Egg-celent!

For eggs that last practically forever, separate them into whites and yolks, then freeze them separately in a lightly oiled ice-cube tray. When frozen, pop them out and store in separate Ziploc bags in the freezer. These frozen eggs are perfect for baking, and will last longer since they're separated.

Leftover Rice

Rice can be stored in the fridge for a longer amount of time if you store a slice of toast on top of it. The toast will absorb excess moisture and keep the rice fluffy and fresh.

Should Produce Be Refrigerated?

Refrigerating your produce can help it keep longer, but not all produce does well in the cooler temperature. The majority of fruits and vegetables handle cold fairly well, but naturally enough, the exceptions are tropical fruits, whose cells are just not used to the cold. Bananas will suffer cell damage and release a skin-browning chemical, avocados don't ripen when stored below 45° F, and citrus fruit will develop brown-spotted skin. These fruits, as well as squash, tomatoes, cucumbers, melons, bell peppers, and pineapples, are best stored at 50° F—so keep them out of the fridge. Most other vegetables, including lettuce, carrots, and cabbage, will do better in your refrigerator.

Garlic, onions, shallots, potatoes, and tomatoes, should never be refrigerated because the cold will cause sprouting, loss of flavor, or conversion of their starch to sugar. Keep these foods out of the refrigerator (at a little cooler than room temperature, if possible) and in a dark cabinet. Humidity is also an important factor, so fruits and vegetables should always be stored in the refrigerator crisper bins, which will prevent them from drying out.

Let Your Produce Breathe

Wrap all produce loosely; air circulating around fruits and vegetables reduces spoilage. A sealed perforated plastic bag is ideal—but instead of buying them at the market, make your own by simply poking several holes in an ordinary sandwich or freezer bag.

A Home for Your Potatoes

Never refrigerate potatoes, because that tends to turn potato starch to sugar. (However, if the potato is removed from the refrigerator and left at room temperature for a few days, the sugar will convert back to starch.) Potatoes will last longer and remain solid longer if they are stored away from light in a cool, dry spot, preferably at 45–50° F. If white potatoes are stored below 40° F, they tend to release more sugar and turn sweet. Air must circulate around potatoes; otherwise, moisture will cause them to decay.

Keep Potatoes for Longer

It is best to purchase potatoes in bulk bins—not in bags, which make it hard to determine which are bruised. If you store fresh ginger with potatoes it will help keep them fresh longer. Half an apple stored with potatoes will stop the sprouting by absorbing moisture before the potato does.

It is always a good idea to line the crisper bins of your refrigerator with a few paper towels to absorb excess moisture. Mold spores love moisture, but the newspaper will keep it away.

Separate Your Onions and Potatoes

Potatoes hate onions...at least until they're cooked together. Onions should never be stored with potatoes because moisture from the onions can cause potatoes to sprout. Onions also release gases that will alter the flavor of a potato.

Open Onions

Yellow and white onions can be kept for a longer amount of time than red ones, as they have a lower sugar content. Store in an open space that's cool and dry, and away from bright light, which can make them bitter. Don't store them anywhere that may become damp.

Keep Onions Fresh

The sugar content in yellow onions makes them spoil quickly if they are stored closely together—who knew? The solution is to store your onions in an old (clean) pair of pantyhose, making knots in the legs so the onions can't touch. It might look a little weird, but it works!

An Onion's Better Half

If you need only half an onion, use the top half first, because the root half will store longer in the refrigerator (it won't sprout).

A Second Life for Your Onion

If you have an onion that becomes pithy and starts to sprout, place it in some soil in a pot on a windowsill and, as it continues to sprout, snip off pieces of the sprouts to use for salad seasoning. These tiny greens are flavorful but not too strong.

Spinach Saving Solutions

Spinach will keep in the refrigerator for 2–3 days, as long as it's stored in a sealed plastic bag. Don't wash it or cut it before you are ready to prepare it, and it will keep longer. If you buy packaged spinach, open the bag when you get home and remove any brown or darkened leaves. If left in the bag, they may cause the rest of the spinach to deteriorate faster. Want to freeze fresh spinach? Remove the stems, blanch the leaves in boiling water for 2 minutes, then run under cold water and dry before you freeze. Removing their stems will allow the leaves to retain more of their moisture. Spinach will keep in the freezer for 10–12 months.

Cucumber Rules

When storing a cucumber, keep it away from apples and tomatoes, which will shorten its life. Cucumbers stay fresh for up to a week, when the water content starts to drop.

Save Your Celery Leaves

Don't throw away celery leaves—while they don't work well with dips, they still have a wonderful flavor. When chopping celery, set the leaves aside on a paper plate, let them dry, and throw them in stuffing, salads, and soups for great extra flavor.

The best way to store celery is to wrap it in aluminum foil and keep it in the fridge. It will last for weeks and weeks.

Avoid Frosted Vegetables

When shopping in the freezer aisle, avoid packages of frozen vegetables that have frost on them. It's a sign that the food has thawed and refrozen, and a percentage of moisture has already been lost. You should also give bags of frozen food a quick squeeze before putting them in your cart. If the food is solid, it has thawed and refrozen, and should be avoided.

The Perfect Use for Unwanted Lettuce Leaves

Don't throw away the outer leaves from a head of lettuce! They come in handy when you need to cover foods in the microwave. You won't have to use up a paper towel, and the leaves will keep your food moist.

Lettuce Abuse?

To make sure it lasts as long as possible, you should remove the innermost core of iceberg lettuce before you store it. An easy (and admittedly fun) way to do this is to hit the lettuce against a hard surface and then twist the core out.

Revive Wilted Greens

To crisp cut-up greens like lettuce, cilantro, or anything else that wilts, soak them in ice water for 15–20 minutes. This also works for limp asparagus and carrots!

Iceberg lettuce remains fresher longer than any other type of lettuce because of its higher water content. Iceberg will keep for 7–14 days, whereas romaine lasts for 6–10 days, and butterhead for only 3–4 days.

Overcooked Overtures

If you've overcooked broccoli, asparagus, or any other vegetable, don't throw it away. Save it for later, when you can cut it up into small pieces and add to a soup, sauce, or stew. They'll cook down even further, so you won't notice anything but the taste.

Give Your Veggies a Haircut

If you've purchased a vegetable with a leafy top, such as beet greens or carrots, remove the green top before you store them in the fridge. The leafy tops will leach moisture from the root or bulb and shorten the vegetable's shelf life.

Storing Corn

Always store corn in a cool, dry location, and keep the ears separated in order to prevent them from becoming moldy. Remember that as it warms up, the sugar in corn converts to starch very quickly. (In fact, when corn is piled high in supermarket bins, the ears on the bottom will be less sweet because of the heat generated by the weight of the ones on top.) To freeze corn, blanch the ears for a minute or two in boiling water, drain, and immediately flush with cold water to stop the cooking. Freeze the ears on a tray, leaving room between them so the kernels aren't crushed and hold their shape. Once the corn is frozen, place the ears in a sealed plastic bag. Frozen corn will keep for one year.

Mushroom Musts

Ever wonder why mushrooms are usually sold in Styrofoam or cardboard containers? Plastic containers tend to keep the mushrooms too wet, and they'll go bad quickly. Fresh mushrooms have a shelf life of only 2–3 days and must be stored in the refrigerator in an open container. The original container or another paper product will work best. Never wash mushrooms before storing them—they'll retain the water and become soggy. If you must keep them for a few days, place a single layer of cheesecloth on top of the container. (If they do become shriveled, they can still be sliced or chopped and used in cooking.) To freeze mushrooms, wipe them off with a damp paper towel, slice them, sauté them in a small amount of butter until they are almost done, allow them to cool, and place them in an airtight plastic bag and freeze. They should keep for 10–12 months.

Separate Drawers

Store fruits and vegetables in separate drawers in your fridge. Even when chilled, fruits give off ethylene gas that shortens the shelf life of other fruit and vegetables by causing them to ripen more quickly.

Making Tomatoes Last

For the best storage, keep tomatoes stem-side down in a cool place. If they are still attached to the stem, remove them from each other and space them so that they're not touching.

High and Dry

The moisture content of fresh berries is high, so make sure to thoroughly dry them before you stick them in the fridge, or wait until you're ready to eat them before you wash them. Otherwise, they can easily rot. Also make sure to store berries, especially strawberries, loosely covered in the refrigerator.

Banana Saver

Never throw out overripe bananas! Stick them in the freezer once they get completely brown, and you can still use them later for banana bread and other baking projects.

Keeping Grapes

Grapes will stay fresh only for three to five days, even if refrigerated. They should be stored, unwashed, in a plastic bag in the coldest part of the refrigerator, but they must be washed very well before eating. If you do wash them before storing, make sure to dry them thoroughly, as they'll easily absorb the water. Grapes don't freeze well because they have a high water content and become mushy when thawed. They can, however, be eaten frozen (they're especially tasty treats), and frozen grapes can be used in cooking. They'll keep in the freezer for about one year.

Long-Lasting Raisins

Raisins will last for several months if they are wrapped tightly in plastic wrap or a plastic bag and kept at room temperature. They will last even longer (up to a year) if you place the plastic bag in the refrigerator.

Easily Make Your Own Bread Crumbs

Don't spend money on store-bought bread crumbs. Set aside a special jar and pour in the crumbs from the bottom of cracker boxes or low-sugar cereal boxes. Also add crumbs from dried-up garlic bread and a few dried herbs and you'll have seasoned bread crumbs!

Keeping Bread

Bread stays fresh for a longer time if you place it in an airtight bag with a stalk of celery. If you are going to freeze a loaf of bread, make sure you include a paper towel in the package to absorb moisture. This will keep the bread from becoming mushy when thawed.

Spice Savers

Both cayenne pepper and paprika are affected by light and heat, and have a shorter shelf life than just about anything else on your spice rack. In fact, take them off your spice rack and store them both in the refrigerator for a longer life.

Never pay for aerosol cooking sprays. Instead, buy a giant jug of vegetable oil and add it to a clean spray bottle as needed. It's the same thing, and will cost you a fraction of the price.

Herbal Remedies

Fresh herbs are a wonderful addition to any dinner, but they go bad quickly and are hard to freeze. To keep herbs fresh longer, loosely wrap them in a damp paper towel, store in a plastic bag, and keep in the vegetable crisper of the refrigerator. If you have more fresh herbs than you can use, hang them upside down to dry. (Tie them together and hang them from a peg.) In about a week, you'll be able to crumble off the leaves. The flavor won't be quite as wonderful as that of fresh herbs, but it will still be much better than commercial dried herbs. Another simple solution is placing chopped, fresh herbs in ice-cube trays. Fill the trays with water and then freeze. When it's time to add herbs to soups and sauces, simply pop as many cubes as you want out of the tray and throw them in the pot.

Tea Saver

Want to get more for your money when it comes to tea? Always buy the loose variety, and then use one-third of what's recommended. Just let the tea steep a little longer, and it will be exactly the same.

Storing Dairy Products

It's better to store milk on an inside shelf—not on the door—toward the back of the refrigerator. Why? All dairy products are very perishable. The optimal refrigeration is actually just over 32° F; however, few

refrigerators are ever set that low or hold that low a temperature. Most home refrigerators remain around 40°, and the temperature rises every time the door is opened. Store cheese near the bottom of the refrigerator, where temperature fluctuations are minimal.

Better Butter

Where you store butter will affect how long it lasts. It will keep for around six months in the freezer, and if you're keeping it in the fridge, it will start to lose its flavor after three weeks. Butter tends to absorb odors and flavors more rapidly than other foods, so make sure to wrap it in a few layers of plastic wrap or foil before storing, especially in the freezer.

Save Those Butter Wrappers

After finishing a stick of unsalted butter, hold on to the wrapper. It'll come in handy when you need to grease a pan: Simply wipe the pan with it. But don't use wrappers from salted butter, since they may cause foods to stick.

For the Last Bit of Shortening

Here's a great tip for the really thrifty. If you want to get all the shortening or lard out of a can, pour 2 cups boiling water into the container and swirl it gently until the fat melts. Refrigerate the container until the shortening solidifies on the water's surface, then just lift or skim it off with a knife blade or a sharp-edged spoon.

Who Knew?

Inside the fridge, margarine quickly absorbs odors from other foods. Make sure you always keep it tightly sealed, and it will keep for 4–5 months in the refrigerator or for a year in the freezer.

Extend the Life of Your Cheese

To keep cheese longer without mold forming, place a piece of paper towel that has been dampened with white vinegar in the bottom of a plastic container with a tight-fitting lid. Add three or four sugar cubes, which will attract the mold if some does form.

Un-Harden Cheese

To soften a piece of hardened (but not moldy) cheese, submerge it in a bowl of buttermilk for one minute. If it's still not soft, cover the dish and refrigerate it overnight.

Revive Moldy Cheese

Believe it or not, cheese with a little mold on it is still perfectly safe to eat once you remove the offending areas. The easiest way to do this is to take a knife or cheese grater, dip it in vinegar, and slice the mold off.

Dip the knife in vinegar after each slice—it kills the mold and prevents it from coming back.

Save Your Rinds

The rinds of hard cheeses like Parmesan are great flavor enhancers for soups. Add a 3-inch square to your next pot of soup, and when you're serving the soup, break up the delicious, melty rind and include it in each bowl. It's completely edible.

Cottage Cheese Care

Because of its high water content, cottage cheese doesn't last as long as other food products in the refrigerator. To extend its life, store it in the container upside down.

Dip Substitution

If your dip recipe calls for sour cream but you have none, cream some cottage cheese in your blender instead. The low-fat variety works best.

For Long-Lasting Marshmallows

In case you've always wondered where to store marshmallows, the answer is the freezer! Just cut them with scissors that have been dipped in very hot water to get them apart.

Sweet Savings

To save money, purchase solid chocolate candy (usually in bunny or Santa form) after major holidays when they've gone on sale. Store the chocolate in the freezer, then shave off bits with a vegetable peeler to use on top of desserts.

● Who Knew?

A chest freezer will remain colder when its door is open than a upright freezer (even though its door is larger than an upright freezer's). This is because cold air is heavier than hot air, and tends to stay put when the door of a chest freezer opens up. Meanwhile, an upright freezer releases most of its cold air the minute the door is opened. Buying a chest freezer can save you money both in energy costs and by giving you a place to store food you've made ahead of time, which will (hopefully) cause you to order in or eat out less.

CHAPTER 19

Kitchen Problems Solved!

For a Clean Cookbook

To keep a cookbook clean, open, and still easy to read while preparing your meal, just place it under a glass pie plate—unless you're making pie, of course!

A "Cookmark"

Making dinner and need something to mark your page in the cookbook? Try using a single strand of raw spaghetti!

Keep Your Remote Clean While Cooking

If you like to channel surf while cooking, place your remote control in a plastic bag or plastic wrap. The buttons will still be visible, and the control will stay clean.

Kill a Kitchen Fire in Two Seconds Flat

If there's a grease fire in a pan, cover the pan immediately with a lid. You'll cut off the oxygen supply and the fire will go out. Baking soda is one of the best fire extinguishers. Always keep an open box next to the stove to dump onto grease fires—and never use water!

Who Knew? Readers' Favorite

If you lost the knob to a pot lid, don't throw out the pot! Place a screw into the hole, with the thread side up, then attach a cork to it.

Stubborn Lid?

Have you ever left a covered pot on the stove only to find that the lid is stuck on? If this happens to you, just try setting the pot over moderate heat for a minute or two. Why? When you cook a food in a covered pot, the air inside the pot increases in pressure, raising the lid ever so slightly so heated air can escape. When you turn off the heat, the air pressure decreases along with the temperature and may become lower than the air pressure outside the pot. This decrease in pressure, along with the water from the steam, creates a vacuum around the lid and seals it tight. The longer the lid is left on, the tighter the seal. Turning the heat back on will increase the air pressure in the pot, loosening the lid's seal.

Open a Stubborn Stuck Jar

An easy way to open a tight jar lid is to cover the top in plastic wrap to create a firm grip. Rubber kitchen gloves or rubber bands work well too. If the jar lid still won't budge, set it in a bowl with a little hot tap water for a few minutes, and then try again. *Still* stuck? Try this trick with a puncture-type can opener: Carefully work the pointed tip under the lid and gently loosen the cap. This should release enough pressure to allow you to open the jar.

Get Rid of Food Smells

If your plastic storage containers smell like garlic, onions, or another potent food, wash them thoroughly, then stuff crumpled newspaper inside before snapping on the lids. In a few days, the smell will be gone.

Keep Wrap in Line

Plastic wrap loves to hug itself. Avoid this by keeping the box in the refrigerator. The cold keeps the wrap from sticking to itself.

Stop Syrup from Running

Frustrated with syrup running down the sides of the bottle, making a disgusting mess? Try this trick: Rub the threads at the neck of the bottle with a small amount of vegetable oil. The oil will prevent the syrup from running and the cap from sticking next time you open it. This also works for molasses and honey containers.

Making Coffee More Drinkable

If you're sensitive to acidity in coffee, but love the pick-me-up in the morning, here's a tip to reduce the acid level: Just add a pinch of baking soda to the drink! You can also use this tip to decrease the acid in other high-acid drinks and foods.

Who Knew?

Don't store fresh-roasted coffee in airtight containers. Fresh-roasted beans are usually packed in bags that are not airtight, which allows the carbon monoxide formed during the roasting process to escape. If the carbon monoxide doesn't escape, the coffee will have a poor taste.

Cure Cloudiness in Iced Tea

Cloudiness is common in brewed iced tea, but it can be easily prevented. Simply let the tea cool to room temperature before refrigerating it. If the tea is still cloudy, try adding a small amount of boiling water to it until it clears up.

A Fizzy Fix

Have you ever had the problem of soda fizzing over the top of an ice-filled glass? Here's a quick trick that will make the cubes fizz less. Put them in the glass first, then rinse them for a few seconds. Pour out the water and add the soda. Since the surface tension of the ice will have changed, then soda won't fizz over.

Make Flat Soda a Thing of the Past

When you pour a warm soft drink over ice cubes, the gas escapes from the beverage at a faster rate because the ice cubes contain more surface for the gas bubbles to collect on, thus releasing more of the carbon dioxide. This is the reason that warm beverages go flat rapidly, and warm drinks poured over ice go flat even faster. To slow down the process, add ice after you've poured the drink and the bubbles have dissipated.

Who Knew?

Ever wonder why ice cubes float? When water freezes, the molecules combine loosely, creating air pockets. When water is in its liquid form, these pockets do not exist, making water denser than ice.

Filtering Your Wine

Red wines that are more than eight years old tend to develop sediment. It's harmless, but it doesn't always look too nice. Get rid of sediment, and any bits of cork, by pouring your wine through a coffee filter and into a decanter before you serve it.

Add Flavor and Fun

Here's a neat trick to get rid of the tiny bit of wine at the end of the bottle. Freeze leftover wine in ice cube trays, then store the cubes in a freezer bag. Use them in wine coolers and any dish that calls for wine.

Salt Shaker Shakeup

When your salt gets sticky in high humidity, keep it flowing freely by adding some raw rice to the shaker to absorb the moisture. Rice absorbs moisture very slowly under these conditions and lasts for a long time.

Who Knew? Readers' Favorite

Make your own version of sippy cups using real glassware you already have. If your glasses are slippery, put a wide rubber band around them so children can get a better grip.

Two Glasses Stuck Together?

The next time you find two drinking glasses stuck together, try this: Fill the top glass with ice water and then place the bottom one in a few inches of hot tap water in the sink. It should only take a few seconds for them to come unstuck.

Unstick Sticky Ice Cube Trays

If your ice cube trays stick to the bottom of the shelf, try placing a piece of waxed paper underneath the tray. Freezing temperatures do not affect waxed paper.

Freezer Freeze Up

A common problem with icemakers is that they freeze up. Next time this happens, just use a blow-dryer to defrost. (For safety's sake, keep the dryer away from any pooling water.) To prevent freezing in the first place, release a few ice cubes every few days.

Microwave Mishap

If a someone accidentally turns on the microwave when it's empty, it can be damaging to the oven. To avoid any problems, just keep a cup of water in the microwave when it is not in use.

Make Cooking with Olive Oil Easier

Olive oil is healthful as oils go, but it has a low smoke point, which means that it will break down rapidly when exposed to heat. You can increase the smoke point of olive oil by adding a small amount of canola oil, which has a very high smoke point. If your recipe calls for tablespoon of olive oil, use 2½ teaspoons olive and ½ teaspoon canola oil and sautéing will be easier.

How to Save a Burned Meal

If you accidentally scorch dinner, set the pot or dish into cold water immediately. This will stop the cooking action and minimize the damage. Carefully remove any unburned food—don't scrape it—then discard whatever is unsalvageable. When you reheat the edible leftovers, set a fresh piece of white bread on top to remove the burnt odor. Alternatively, there's always pizza delivery!

Burned a Roast?

There are few kitchen disasters more disheartening than burning a roast. But there's help! If you burn or scorch a roast, remove it from the pan and cover it with a towel dampened with hot water for about five minutes, which will stop the cooking. Then remove or scrape off any burnt areas with a sharp knife, and put the roast back in the oven to reheat if necessary.

Ham Too Salty?

A little salt in ham is a good thing, but if your ham slices are too salty, place them in a dish of low-fat milk for 20 minutes before heating, then rinse them off in cold water and dry them with paper towels. The ham won't pick up the taste of the milk, but will taste much less salty.

● Who Knew?

Ever cooked a cut of meat that turned out gray, and wondered why? Meats may turn grayish in color if they are cooked in too small a pot. Overcrowding tends to generate excess steam—so, for a nice brown crust, give your meat some room to breathe.

Defrost in a Flash

The best way to thaw turkey is on a shallow baking sheet in the refrigerator, in its original packaging, allowing 24 hours for every five pounds of bird. But if it's Thanksgiving morning and you've forgotten to stick the bird in the fridge, the fastest, safest method of thawing frozen poultry fast is to place it—still wrapped in plastic—in a bowl (or bucket) of cold water. Check the water regularly and change it as the water warms up—you should never use hot water, as it will promote bacterial growth.

Zap Microwave Odors

Fresh fish is a summertime treat, but fresh fish smell in your microwave is not. Get rid fish or other microwave odors by putting a quartered lemon or a small bowl of vanilla in your microwave for a minute or two on high.

Get Rid of That Fish Smell

If you've been preparing fish and want to remove the smell from your hands, try washing them with water and a bit of toothpaste. Lemon juice and a little salt also work well.

Removing Kitchen Cooking Odors

The odor from cooking fish and other pungent foods can linger over your kitchen for hours. To make it quickly disappear, place a bowl of white vinegar on the counter near the stove while cooking. The vinegar will absorb the smell.

Stop Separation Anxiety in Gravies

Does your gravy separate? If so, simply add a pinch or two of baking soda to emulsify the fat globules in a matter of seconds.

Gravy Savers

Gravy is so delicious, yet so easy to mess up. To help prevent lumpy gravy, add a pinch of salt to the flour before using any liquid. If lumps persist, use your blender to smooth it out. If your gravy burns, just stir in a teaspoon of peanut butter to cover up the burnt flavor without altering the meaty taste.

If you add wine to a soup or sauce that already contains milk or cream, it may curdle; adding the wine and cooking it briefly before you add the dairy product should help prevent this.

Skimming the Fat without the Refrigerator

You can de-fat soup and gravy easily even if you don't have time to refrigerate it. Remove it from the heat for 5–10 minutes. Put four or five ice cubes in a piece of cheesecloth and swirl it around in the soup or gravy. Fat is attracted to the cold, and should stick to the cheesecloth. It will also be attracted to lettuce leaves—stir a few leaves into the soup for a few minutes, and then discard them. Another method is to add a slice of fresh white bread on top of the fat for a few seconds. After the bread absorbs the fat, it should be disposed of—if you leave the bread on the soup too long, it will fall apart.

Too-Salty Solutions

If your soup or stew is too salty, use one of these methods to make it less so. Add a can of peeled tomatoes or a small amount of brown sugar if it won't affect the taste; or stir in a slice or two of raw apple or potato, let simmer a few minutes, then discard the apple or potato.

Egg Separation Made Easy

If you don't have an egg separator, the easiest way to separate the yolks from the whites when necessary is to crack them into a funnel. The whites slide out, leaving the yolk behind.

It's easy to tell whether an egg has been hard-boiled: Spin it. If it wobbles, it's raw—the yolk sloshes from one end of the egg to the other. Hard-cooked eggs spin evenly, because the yolk is held in place by the cooked egg white. Reduce your risk of spinning an egg right off the counter by adding a drop or two of food coloring to the water when you boil them. It will dye the shells so you can tell the difference.

Don't OD on Mayo

Too much mayonnaise or salad dressing can ruin a dish. To fix the problem, try adding breadcrumbs to absorb the excess.

Unstick Your Rice

If your rice sticks together when you cook it, next time add a teaspoon of lemon juice to the water when boiling. Your sticky problem will be gone!

Rice Repair

If you burned the rice, fear not! It's white bread to the rescue. Get rid of the scorched taste by placing a slice of fresh white bread on top of the rice, while it's still hot, and covering it for a few minutes.

Cracked wheat can be a nutritious substitute for rice in many dishes. It is prepared by toasting whole-wheat berries (the bran and germ are kept intact), which are then broken into coarse, medium, and fine fragments.

Pizza Cutting Prescription

Pizza cutters are great—until they start to get dull. One of easiest ways to cut a pizza is to use clean scissors with long blades—you can cut from top and bottom, and you can cut through the pizza quickly. Make sure they are sharp and only used for food.

A Plan for Pizza-Making

Making pizzas at home is a great way to save money and get the kids involved in making dinner. But homemade pizzas often lack the crispness of pizzeria pies. Here's one tip that should help: Add the cheese before the tomato sauce. Cheese has a lower water content than tomatoes do, so the crust won't get as soggy.

From Whole to Chopped

Your market has only canned whole tomatoes, and you need chopped! Don't mess with taking out each tomato and making a mess on your cutting board. Instead, simply insert a clean pair of scissors into the can and snip.

Insta-Peel for Tomatoes

Need to quickly peel tomatoes for a recipe? The easiest way is to place them in a pot of boiling water for a minute. The skins will practically fall off.

Keep Tomatoes from Staining Your Plastic

Plastic containers are perfect for keeping leftovers and sauces, but tomato sauce will often stain clear plastic. To keep this from happening, simply spray the container with non-stick cooking spray before pouring in tomato-based sauces. To remove a plastic stain, cover the area with mustard and leave overnight.

Easing the Acidity of Tomatoes

Some people are unable to eat spaghetti sauces and other tomato-based foods because of their high acid content. Adding chopped carrots and cooking them with tomato dishes will reduce the acidity without affecting the taste.

Who Knew?

The only benefit of homemade spaghetti sauce isn't just the taste. Commercial sauces are almost always much higher in fat and calories.

No-Sugar Sweetener

Carrots are also a natural sweetener. To sweeten a soup, stew, or sauce without adding sugar, stir in a small amount of pureed carrots. Use one of the sweeter carrot varieties.

For a Guacamole Emergency!

If you bought a whole bunch of avocados for your guacamole and they're still not ripe enough to use, you can use this tip—which isn't ideal, but will do the trick. Prick the skin of each avocado in several places, then microwave it on high for 40–70 seconds, flipping it over halfway through. This won't ripen the avocado, but it will soften it enough that you'll be able to mash it with ripe avocados and your guests won't notice.

Keep Guacamole Looking Fresh

You may look good with a tan, but your guacamole sure doesn't! To keep the avocados from oxidizing (which causes the brown color), cut the avocados with a silver or stainless steel knife, and leave the pit in the dip (until serving). Sprinkle lemon juice on the surface of the dip, and cover tightly with plastic wrap until you're ready to eat.

Reduce Green Odors

Kale, cabbage, and collard greens are delicious to eat, but can sometimes smell stinky when they're being prepared. Make sure not to overcook them, which will make them release more odors, and place a few unshelled pecans in the saucepan while cooking, which will help absorb any scents.

Peeled Potato Prescription

You've managed to talk your kids into helping you with tonight's scalloped potatoes, but now the potatoes are peeled long before you need them! To keep peeled potatoes from discoloring, place them in a bowl of cold water with a few drops of white vinegar added in, then refrigerate. Drain before cooking and add a small amount of sugar to the cooking water to revive some of the lost flavor.

Did you know potatoes can remove some stains from your hands? Just rub raw potato slices against the stain under water.

Keep Fruit Looking Fresh

Even though it doesn't affect the taste, it's still disappointing to unveil your fruit salad only to discover a thin layer of brown oxidation all over the fruit. A common method for keeping cut fruit looking fresh is to add a bit of lemon juice. However, an even more effective method is to fill a spray bottle with water and a few dissolved vitamin C tablets (usually available near the counter or cold-remedy section of your drug store). Spray this on the cut fruit and not only will it not turn brown, you'll be getting added vitamins!

The Brown Bag Trick

Fruit normally gives off ethylene gas, which hastens ripening. Some fruits give off more gas than others and ripen faster. Other fruits are picked before they are ripe and need a bit of help. If an unripe fruit is placed in a brown paper bag, the ethylene gas it gives off does not dissipate into the air but is trapped and concentrated, causing the fruit to ripen faster. To get it to ripen even more quickly, add a ripe apple— one of those ethylene-rich fruits.

Perking Up Apples

If apples are dry or bland, slice them and put them in a dish, and then pour cold apple juice over them and refrigerate for 30 minutes. OK, so it's kind of a cheat, but it will make sure picky eaters get their nutrients!

Apple Botox

To prevent baked apples from wrinkling, peel the top third or cut a few slits in the skin to allow for expansion.

Making Jam?

If you add a small pat of butter when cooking fruits for preserves and jellies, there will be no foam to skim off the top. The fat acts as a sealant and prevents the air from rising and accumulating on top as foam.

Juice for Juice

If you've been cooking with berries and your hands are stained, try removing the berry juice stains with a bit of lemon juice.

Raisin Rejuvenation

Sad-looking raisins? To plump them up to perfection, place them a small baking dish with a little water, cover, and bake in a preheated 325° oven for 6–8 minutes. Or, pour boiling water over the raisins and let them stand for 10–15 minutes.

Chopping Dried Fruits

Raisins and other dried fruits won't stick to your knife (or anything) if you first soak them in cold water for 10 minutes.

Quick-Rising Solutions

It's not always a good idea to artificially quicken the amount of time it takes your bread dough to rise (the flavor of the bread may not be as full), but if you're in a time crunch, it's always nice to have a back-up plan. To speed whole-wheat bread dough's rising time, add one tablespoon of lemon juice to the dough as you are mixing it. When it comes to other breads, a little heat does wonders when it comes to cutting down on rising time. Set the dough (either in a bowl or a loaf pan) on a heating pad set on medium, or over the pilot light on a gas stove. You can also use the microwave to help speed up the rising process by as much as one-third. Set ½ cup hot water in the back corner of the microwave. Place the dough in a well-greased microwavable bowl and cover it with plastic wrap, and then cover the plastic wrap with a damp towel. With the power level set at 10 percent, cook the dough for 6 minutes, and then let it rest for 4 to 5 minutes. Repeat the procedure if the dough has not doubled its size.

Slow Down Browning Baked Goods

If you're having a problem with bread browning too fast, set a dish of water on the oven rack just above the bread. The added humidity in the oven will slow down the browning. This will work with cakes as well.

Dishes containing sour cream must be reheated slowly to prevent the cream from separating. This is why sour cream is normally added toward the end of a dish's preparation.

Double-Decker

If you don't have an insulated or a thick baking sheet, there's a simple solution: Try baking the cookies on two sheets, stacked one on top of the other. It will eliminate burned bottoms caused by a too-thin pan.

Rust Remover

To treat rust on metal baking dishes and cookware, sprinkle powdered laundry detergent on the spot, then scour with the cut side of half a raw potato.

Prevent a Pudding Problem

Laying a sheet of wax paper directly onto a custard or pudding while it is still hot will keep a layer of skin from developing.

Is Your Brown Sugar Lumpy?

Brown sugar loses moisture rather quickly and develops lumps easily. To soften hardened sugar, put it in the microwave with a slice of fresh white bread or half an apple, cover the dish tightly and heat for 15–20 seconds; let it stand five minutes before using. The moisture from the bread or apple will produce enough steam to soften the sugar without melting it. Store brown sugar in the freezer to keep it from getting lumpy in the first place.

More Tips for Lumpy Sugar

Granulated sugar clumps less than brown sugar, but it's still easy to get sugar lumps. Keep this from happening by sticking a few salt-free crackers in the canister to absorb the moisture; replace the crackers every week.

Soften Hardened Marshmallows

If you find an old bag of marshmallows that have hardened, add a slice of very fresh white bread or half an apple to the bag to soften them. Unfortunately, it's not a quick fix: You might need to leave the bag for one or two days until the marshmallows absorb the moisture.

Who Knew? Readers' Favorite

Are your popcorn kernels too pooped to pop? It's probably because they have lost too much moisture, but they can be revived. Soak the kernels in water for five minutes, then dry them off and try again. Or freeze them overnight and pop them when frozen.

When Movie Night Goes Wrong

If you've ever burned popcorn in your microwave, you know that it stinks, and the smell likes to permeate the entire household. Make it smell fresh again by stuffing the microwave with crumpled newspaper for a few hours. Remove the paper, and boil water and baking soda in a glass bowl for five minutes, and the smell should be gone.

PART THREE

Health & Beauty

Keeping the house looking perfect almost seems easy when it comes to keeping ourselves looking good! But beauty doesn't always have to be a "regimen." Sometimes, all it takes are a few simple tips to keep your clothes as good as new, your skin looking like you're 20 years old, and your make-up flawless. The tips in this section will give you easy ways to rejuvenate your skin and hair, tell you how to make the most out of your make-up, teach how you to use your wardrobe to help your figure, let your clothes last longer, and give you easy ways to better your health using all-natural remedies. So get ready to take a relaxing bath and bring our book with you!

CHAPTER 20

Better Beauty

Don't Tear Your Hair

When hair is damp or wet it is much weaker and more easily damaged. Always treat wet hair carefully, and use a wide-toothed comb to straighten out tangles rather than a brush, which can create split ends.

Hot Honey Hair

Give your hair and scalp a treat with an organic conditioner made from honey and olive oil. Mix equal parts together and warm in the microwave. Then apply the mixture to clean, towel-dried hair, and wrap in a warm towel for 20 minutes before washing out. Your hair will be smooth, shiny, and ultra-soft.

Cold Shine

Extra-shiny hair starts in the shower! Finish your final rinse with a blast of the most freezing cold water you can bear. It closes the hair cuticles so that light bounces off them, resulting in super-shiny locks.

● Who Knew?

Many hair products contain alcohol, which can dry out your hair and scalp. If your hair is dyed, it will also make it duller. Look carefully at the ingredients before buying a hair product and stay away from alcohol!

Restore with Massage

It turns out that the person washing your hair at the salon is onto something! When you apply shampoo or conditioner, take a few moments to give yourself a slow fingertip scalp massage. Using gentle circular motions and a reasonable amount of pressure pushing down onto the scalp, you will boost blood circulation around the follicles and stimulate re-growth.

Condition with Care

Some leave-in conditioners are unsuitable for fine hair. These conditioners coat the hair to protect it, but they can weigh it down and make it dull and greasy (and very difficult to style). Wash-out conditioners generally suit all hair types better.

Protect Your Hair From Beach Damage

Spending a windy summer day out on the beach? Strong winds on a sandy beach can cause as much damage to your hair as the sun, so to protect your locks run some leave-in conditioner into your hair before you go. Choose one that contains vitamin B5, which will nourish and protect your hair.

Tips for Thin Hair

Hair naturally thins out as part of the aging process, as the number of follicles capable of growing hairs gradually declines. A straight part with hair that just hangs down from it will emphasize the problem, so ask your stylist to create a style that incorporates color and texture.

Help a Dandruff Problem

The shiny white scales that separate from the scalp and collect on the hair and shoulders (otherwise known as dandruff) can be decreased by changing your diet. Increase your intake of raw foods that are high in enzymes (fruit, vegetables, and nuts), and if your dandruff still doesn't improve, try swallowing two spoonfuls of flax seed oil a day.

Greasy hair? Get rid of excess hair oil with a weekly treatment of cold peppermint tea. Simply wash your hair as usual, then pour the cooled tea over your hair. It will get rid of grease, as well as make your hair smell fresh and minty all day long!

Kitchen Color Corrector

If your blonde hair turns a strange shade of green after a summer spent swimming in chlorinated pools, comb tomato ketchup through your hair and leave for 20 minutes to neutralize the color. Wash and condition as usual and your hair will be a beautiful blonde again!

Another Cure for Chlorinated Hair

If your hair has changed color from too much chlorine, here's another way to fix it. Crush 10 aspirin tablets into a cup of warm water, then work the solution through your hair. Let it sit for about 15 minutes, then wash out, and your hair should be back to its old self.

Scrub Away from the Face!

Don't be tempted to use a body scrub on the delicate skin of your face. Body scrubs contain larger, rougher granules than facial exfoliants, and they'll irritate and inflame the sensitive skin on your face.

Beware of Overdoing It

Over-cleansing is a major cause of sensitive skin, as it strips the skin's underlying layers of its natural protective properties. Make sure you use a cleanser that's right for your skin type and don't wash your face too often—if you notice red spots or rough patches, cleanse less regularly or try applying a moisturizer afterward.

Wake Up Your Face!

In the morning, your face can look pale and puffy because of the natural nocturnal slow-down in the body. When putting on your moisturizer, take the opportunity to gently massage all the muscles in your face to wake up the lymphatic system and jump start the circulation.

A Workout for Your Face

To tighten a wobbly chin area, push your lips tightly together and make a wide grimace to contract your lower facial muscles. Hold for three seconds and repeat 20 times each day.

Get Smooth with Soy

Soy proteins can help make skin temporarily smoother by improving firmness and elasticity if applied regularly. Look for them as ingredients in new "high-tech" face creams.

The 30-Second Skin Reviver

Whether you just need to wake up, or freshen up your skin, here's the perfect 30-second skin reviver. Place a fresh hand towel under steaming hot water (not boiling—the hottest you get out of your tap is fine), then cover your entire face with it for 30 seconds. Then use the towel or a warm, wet washcloth to buff your T-zone area (chin, nose, and forehead). For a finishing touch, splash cold water all over your face to leave your pores tight and tingling.

Forget the Botox and grab the bananas instead! You can make an all-natural (and inexpensive) moisturizing face mask using bananas. Simply mash up a few of them into a paste, then smooth onto your face and neck. (You can also use avocados, but they're much more expensive!) Let it set (20 minutes should do it), then rinse with cold water. Your skin will look and feel softer.

Two Minute Face-Lift

If you skin is looking a little sallow, whip up this simple face mask: Combine 1 egg yolk and 2 teaspoons lemon juice. Rub onto your face and leave for two minutes, and it will have a tightening effect that will leave your skin feeling fresh and glowing.

Give Skin a Feast

Skin is the last organ to get the benefits of the good things you eat, so often there's precious little nutrients left, even if your diet is fantastic. To make sure your skin gets the nourishment it needs, choose face treatments that are high in such essential minerals as calcium, magnesium, and zinc to give it a boost.

Taming Unruly Brows

It's happened to the best of us: You look in the mirror and notice that your eyebrows are out of control! When this happens to you, a little dab of petroleum jelly—or even lip gloss in a pinch—can help keep curly hairs in a sleek, sophisticated line. Alternatively, use a little hairspray sprayed on your eyebrow brush to smooth them into place.

Hairspray is basically a resin dissolved in a volatile solvent or alcohol. When you spray it on your hair, the solvent evaporates rapidly, leaving a thin layer of plastic. Don't believe it? Try this experiment: Coat a mirror with a thick layer of hair spray and let it dry for a minute or two. You should be able to peel off the layer in one thin sheet.

Goodbye to Puffy Eyes

To combat puffy eyes, place slices of cucumber on them. It may seem like an old wives' tale, but cucumbers have a mild anti-inflammatory action. To make your experience even more enjoyable, keep the cucumber in the fridge until you're ready to use it. The coolness will feel wonderful on your eyelids, and the cold will help further restrict blood vessels, making puffiness go down.

Herbal Eye Treatment

Reduce puffy or swollen eyes with a green tea compress. Dip cotton wool into the green tea, drain off excess moisture, and then dab gently around the eye area. This will help to tighten the skin around the eyes.

Who Knew?

There are no oil glands in the skin directly beneath and above the eyes, which is why the skin in those areas has a tendency to get fine lines and wrinkles. Make sure to moisturize regularly in this area to keep your skin looking fresh and young.

Farewell, Rough Lips

Get rid of dead skin on your lips with an all-natural exfoliating rub made from ingredients in your own kitchen. Mix a drop of sesame or olive oil with brown sugar, then rub the delicious mixture gently over lips to remove flaky skin. Finish by applying petroleum jelly.

Brush-Up

Though we usually go with the cheapest option, when it comes to make-up brushes it's worth it to invest in high quality, and good brushes will make application easier, faster, and more polished-looking. Brushes should always have bristles that feel soft against the skin. It's important to wash them at least every three months with a mild liquid soap.

Quick Make-Up Removal

You should never leave make-up on overnight, as it can dry out your skin (and leave marks on your pillow!). One of the quickest ways to remove make-up is with a pre-moistened wipe, but skip the expensive "make-up removal wipes" and keep of stash of baby wipes near the sink instead. The next time you come home after a late night, make sure to rub a wipe over your face before you hit the sack.

Do It Up in the Daylight

When applying your make-up in the morning, always apply it under natural light, as your skin will look drastically different under the light from your bathroom bulb. Set up a magnifying mirror near a window with a good source of natural light, and make sure that shading is properly blended for the most natural-looking face.

Formula for Foundation

Most people use far more foundation than they need—and since it's one of the most expensive types of make-up, that's money down the drain! To make sure you're using the proper amount, simply apply one dot to each of your cheeks, your forehead, and your nose, then blend thoroughly. Don't be afraid to leave some areas bare.

Keeping It Light

Summer beauty requires a lighter touch. To keep your skin tone looking fresh and even, stash away your foundation and just use a tinted moisturizer with an SPF of 15 or higher to cover the occasional blemish and give protection from the sun.

Shapely Brows

Defining your brow line with a pencil and a little plucking is a great way to open up your face and make your eyes sparkle. But how do you know where your brows should begin and end? To determine exactly where your brow should begin, imagine a vertical line or hold a make-up pencil straight alongside one nostril. Where the pencil lands by your brow is where it should begin. To work out where the brow should end, imagine a line from the outside of your nostril to the outer corner of your eye, then extend it out to your brow.

Trick Lips

To give the illusion of a fuller upper lip, dab a tiny touch of pale, iridescent sheen in the center of the lips, then rub to blend in with the rest of your lipstick. This will highlight your cupid's bow (the curvy portion of your lips), making it appear bigger than it is.

Make Your Teeth Look Whiter

Choose your lipstick color carefully! Shades of purple or blue-based pinks can make teeth look whiter, while orangey browns will make them look yellowish.

Ditch a Double Chin

If a "double chin" is driving you nuts, use a little make-up to hide it. When applying powder or foundation to your face, use a slightly darker shade under your chin, which will make it appear to recede. Blend towards the back of the jawline to add definition. And when posing for pictures, stick your chin out as much as possible to stretch out the skin in the area.

Boost Your Cleavage

If you're wearing a low-cut top, use a bit of powder to give your skin an even color and smooth appearance below your neck. Using a smidgen of blush down your cleavage line will add a "shadow," making your bust look a bit larger.

How 'Bout a Buff?

If your manicure usually ends up chipped, consider buffing your nails as an alternative. An expensive nail buffer can bring your nails to a natural shine that is sure to get noticed. Just make sure to only buff your nails once a week. Over-buffing weakens the nails by taking away their top layer and making them more porous.

Who Knew? Readers' Favorite

Once a month, cover your hands in petroleum jelly or thick hand cream, and slip them into some soft cotton gloves for the night. In the morning, all the cream will have been absorbed, leaving you with the smoothest, softest hands you've ever had. You can also soften your feet the same way (just use socks rather than gloves).

Give Your Hands a Break

Because the skin on your hands is thin and endlessly ravaged by the elements, keep them as dry as much as possible—never walk out of a restroom with wet hands. Water left on hands will evaporate, which will dry them out and can even cause them to turn red. If you're especially prone to dry hands, look for a hand cream that contains lanolin.

Moisturize Before You Get Dirty

Slather on a heavy layer of hand moisturizer before painting or doing other dirty chores. It will prevent dirt and paint from seeping into your skin, making clean-up easier. White soap under your nails will help, too.

Smell Bleach on Your Skin?

Bleach is an awesome household-cleaning tool, but it has one potential downside: It smells. To eliminate the smell of bleach from your hands, wash them in warm water and toothpaste. The white, non-gel variety works best.

Fix a Nail Polish Disaster

If you've just dumped nail polish on your floor or table, don't despair. You may be able to remove it using shaving cream. Using a soft cloth, rub shaving cream on the nail polish, leave for several minutes, and wipe off. Just make sure to test an inconspicuous area of the surface first, to make sure the shaving cream won't harm it.

Clear Up a Contact Catastrophe

Lost a contact lens and can't seem to find it anywhere? Turn off the lights and turn on a flashlight. Sweep it over the area where you lost it and the lens will reflect the light.

Feet Freshener

Smelly feet? To easily freshen them, simply rub a few slices of lemon over them. It will also help prevent athlete's foot.

Callus Cure

To remove hard calluses from your feet, try this old-fashioned but effective remedy: Grind a few aspirin tablets into a paste with equal parts lemon juice and water. Apply it to the calluses, then wrap your feet in a hot towel, cover in plastic bags, and stay off your feet for 30 minutes. When you unwrap your feet, the calluses will be soft and ready to be filed off with a nail file or pumice stone.

Homemade Bubble Bath

You don't need expensive bath gels to get a luxurious bubble bath. To make your own bubble bath, simply place soap slivers in a mesh drawstring bag. (To get soap slivers, use a vegetable peeler on a sturdy bar of soap.) Attach the bag to the tap while the water is running. For even more fragrance, put a couple of drops of favorite essential oil in the bag, or herbs like rosemary and thyme.

The Best Bath

Make your bath time work for you by adding a pound of Epsom salts to the water. Epsom salts are made from the mineral magnesium sulfate, which draws toxins from the body, sedates the nervous system, and relaxes tired muscles. Goodbye expensive bath salts!

For an inexpensive, luxuriously fragrant bath oil, mix sunflower oil with either crushed lavender or rose petals (or both). Let it stand for a few days before using it.

A Luxurious Bath Treat

You can literally bathe in your favorite perfume by making your own scented bath oil. Just add a few drops of perfume to a quart of baby oil, shake well, and add to your bath.

Perfume Storage Secret

Perfume is very volatile—the fragrance breaks down rapidly when exposed to heat and air. If you're not going to use the entire bottle within 30 days, store it in the refrigerator to extend its life.

Just a Dab Will Do You

Do you find your perfume fading after a few hours? To make it last longer, rub a small amount of petroleum jelly onto your skin before you dab on your favorite scent.

What's the difference between perfume, cologne, and eau de toilette? The main variant is the concentration of the compounds that are responsible for the aroma of each of these products. Perfumes are produced with the highest concentrations, and that's why they last longer. Colognes contain less of the same compound and more fillers, and eau de toilette, or toilet water, is just diluted cologne.

Exfoliation Made Easy

Instead of buying expensive sea salt and other body exfoliants, get in the habit of using a loofah or soft brush each day to slough off dead skin cells and encourage new regeneration. Rubbing with a loofah or brush will also help your circulation, with will not only wake you up in the morning, but will help your skin look smoother, as better blood flow helps disperse fatty deposits.

Homemade Exfoliant

For a super-smoothing skin exfoliant, mix a handful of Epsom salts with a tablespoon of olive oil and rub over wet skin to cleanse, exfoliate, and soften the rough spots. Rinse off well for a polished finish. If you don't have Epsom salts, use the coarsest table salt you can find.

A Cream You Can't Live Without

Available online and in health food and vitamin shops, horse chestnut cream is said to diminish the tiny red veins that appear on your cheeks and nose as you age. Skin becomes thinner and loses some of its collagen as you get older, and horse chestnut cream improves blood circulation and will make these annoying veins disappear.

Take a Deep Breath

Make your nighttime lotion regimen even more effective by taking five deep breaths to boost levels of oxygen to the skin before smoothing on your cream.

Overnight Hydration

During the night, the skin rests and repairs itself after the stresses of the day, so nothing's worse than waking up to dry skin in the winter. Use a humidifier or place a damp towel over your radiator at night to replenish moisture in the air and keep your skin hydrated. This helps to humidify the air around you, and reduces excessive water loss from your skin.

Who Knew? Readers' Favorite

Brighten dull and sallow skin with a little help from your kitchen! Mix equal parts lemon juice and milk, then rub into your skin with a soft cloth and leave on for five minutes before rinsing. Your skin will feel tingly fresh and look rejuvenated.

Sweet as Honey

Soft, supple skin is as easy as using a little honey. Simply apply honey straight from the jar on to skin that has been moistened with warm water. Leave for up to 30 minutes, then rinse off .

Get Help from AHAs

When looking for an anti-aging product, make sure to keep an eye out for alpha-hydroxy acids (AHAs). These organic chemicals are derived from fruit-bearing plants, hence they're often called "fruit acids." Thought to help generate new collagen, making skin firmer and plumper, they also dissolve the "glue" that binds dead cells, allowing the old ones to be washed or cleansed away while revealing younger cells. AHAs are great for your skin—find the least expensive product you can find that contains these wonder acids!

The Secret to Smooth Skin

If you want skin that's as smooth as a tomato, then eat one! Tomatoes contain lycopene, a skin-friendly antioxidant that is also thought to reduce the risk of cancer. Cooking tomatoes makes lycopene more readily absorbable by the body, so choose tomato sauces over the raw fruits in salads.

Papaya Power

Papaya contains the papain enzyme, a natural, nonabrasive botanical that dissolves dead skin cells, which makes it a great ingredient for face masks and exfoliations. It deeply cleanses without stripping, leaving dull skin smoother and more refined. If you find papaya on sale, buy extra and cut up to rub over your skin.

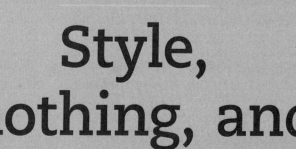

CHAPTER 21

Style, Clothing, and Jewelry Tips

Is Your Look Working for You?

Many women (and some men) love having long locks, but a thick, solid curtain of glossy hair can overwhelm your face and make your skin look dull and tired. If you have long hair, make sure to cut some shorter layers from underneath to produce movement around your face and let light shine through.

Uplift Your Look

One of the narrowest areas on a woman's body is across the ribs, just beneath the bustline, yet large or droopy breasts can hide this area. Make your figure look more like an hourglass by wearing a supportive, push-up style bra, which will help make the line from rib to hip look more elongated and shapely.

Who Knew?

Research has shown that 80 percent of women wear the wrong bra size. A good-fitting bra shouldn't be too tight or ride up in back, and the cups should be big enough to be supportive. Ask at a lingerie shop or department store if they offer free, professional fittings. You may be surprised to find you've been buying the wrong size your whole life.

Embrace Your Curves

If you're not thin, you've been cursed to disfavorably compare yourself to movie stars for the rest of your life. The good news is that you also have curves that those women would kill for. Celebrate your womanly body by wearing clothes that show it off by hugging your sides. Wrap dresses and fitted clothes are always preferable to baggy clothing, which just hangs from your widest point and does nothing to show off your good points (and everybody has at least one good point)!

Tummy Trick

Most of us have a little more tummy than we'd like. Luckily, if you're a woman, you can help disguise it with the help of tailored pants. When shopping for dress pants, choose a look that has a flat front and a side zipper, which won't add any bulk to your front.

Single-Breasted Suits Us

As gravity (and middle-age) takes its toll, a layer of fat may be making its way around your midsection. We'll let you decide whether to hit the gym, but when you hit the store, stay away from double-breasted jackets. Always choose single-breasted suits, as two sets of buttons make the body appear wider.

The Kids May Be Onto Something

You may scoff that low-waisted pants are for teenagers only, but they can have their benefits. Jeans and pants that sit between the hips and the waist can help hide extra weight, as higher-waisted pants clamp the middle tummy, making it appear larger and highlighting a lack of waist.

Who Knew? Readers' Favorite

Add a little extra length to your legs by always wearing pants that cover the top of your shoes and just skim the floor.

Let Your Feet Breathe

It's tempting to buy the smallest pair of shoes your feet can fit into, but too-tight shoes can cause corns, calluses, bunions, and—later on down the line—bone spurs and hammer toe. Make sure your shoes are the right size, and if possible, don't wear the same pair of shoes two days in a row.

Shoelace Trick

Having trouble keeping your (or your kids') shoelaces tied? Shoelaces are more likely to stay tied if you dampen them with water first.

Steam Away Smoke

To remove a smoky smell from your clothes, fill your bathtub with hot water and add 1 cup white vinegar. Then just hang the clothes above the steaming water, and the smoke smell will dissipate in about an half hour. Ah, vinegar—is there anything it can't do?

Iron On Your Favorite Fragrance

This smart tip will make your clothes smell wonderful. Add a drop of perfume to the water in your steam iron, then iron your shirts, underwear, lingerie—everything! You'll enjoy your favorite perfume wherever you go.

Buttons Equal Cents!

Here's a tip for the thrifty (and clever): Always remove buttons before discarding a garment. They will come in handy later!

Smoother Sewing

If a pin or needle will not easily penetrate an article, this little household trick will make sewing a cinch: Simply stick the pin into a bar of soap to make it nice and slippery.

Static Trick

One easy way to remove static cling is to run the long part of a wire hanger over the garment. If you've suffered any skirt-stuck-to-panty-hose embarrassment, run the hanger between your skirt and the panty hose. Shape the hanger to fit inside pant legs or under a dress or skirt.

Prevent Pantyhose Runs

Weird but true: Freezing panty hose can keep them from running. Before wearing a pair of nylons for the first time, stick them in the freezer overnight. The cold strengthens the fibers, which will keep them from running.

The Zipper Fix

Got a zipper that won't stay closed? Spray it lightly and carefully with hairspray after zipping up.

Baseball Cap Cleanse

Wash a baseball cap on the top rack of your dishwasher, and remove while still wet. Then, place the cap over a bowl to regain its shape, and dry it away from direct sunlight.

A Shave for Your Sweater

Next time you replace your disposable razor, keep the old one. Gently "shaving" your sweater will quickly and easily get rid of pills and lint.

Sweater Stretched?

If cuffs or necklines of woolen sweaters are stretched out of shape, dip them in hot water and dry with a blow dryer. They should shrink back to their original size.

Who Knew? Readers' Favorite

If your favorite cashmere or angora sweater is looking a little worn, put it in a plastic bag and place it in the freezer for half an hour. The cold causes the fibers to expand, making your sweater look new again! Who knew there was such a thing as sweater cryogenics?

Out, Damned Moth, Out, I Say!

Cedar is an effective, natural solution to fend off those pesky clothes moths—and it smells great too. If your cedar blocks or cedar chests have lost their aroma (along with those moth-repelling powers), restore it with this simple trick: Rub the wood lightly with fine sandpaper. Repeat every season to make sure your closets are moth-free.

Your Clothes Need Air Too

To eliminate moth damage or mildew from your wool sweaters and down jackets, wash the garments before storing, and never keep them in plastic bags or airtight containers. Your clothes need air, so consider a trunk made of wicker, cedar, or rattan, and avoid hot attics or damp basements.

No-Wrinkle Packing Technique

When packing for vacation, place your pants in the bottom of the suitcase, with half of them hanging over the side. Place the rest of your clothes on top, then fold the pants back over on top of the clothes. When you unpack, your pants won't need to be pressed.

For Fresh-Smelling Luggage

When you return home from your summer vacation, throw a few dryer sheets in your suitcases before you put them away. The sheets will prevent any musty odors from festering while the bags are stored.

Kill Bad BO with Dryer Sheets

Don't underestimate the power of a single fabric softener sheet. Just stick one in your gamy old gym bag and in each of your musty sneakers—your funk will be extinguished in no time!

Who Knew? Readers' Favorite

Do your shoes smell? Fill a clean sheer stocking with tea leaves, then stuff it in your shoes. The smell will vanish in a day or two. Continue storing your shoes with the tea leaves to prevent smelly shoes in the future.

Reboot Your Boots

Keep your boots looking their best by storing them with empty wine or soda bottles inside. It will keep your boots upright and help them maintain their shapes.

White Sneakers That Stay White

After purchasing new cotton sneakers, spray them with spray starch to help them resist stains. The starch will repel grease and dirt, keeping them whiter!

Been Out in the Rain?

You should never attempt to dry your shoes with a hairdryer, as the heat can make the rubber in the shoes soft and allow your shoes to become deformed. If you need dry shoes fast, use the blower end of a vacuum cleaner hose instead.

The Magic of Lemon Juice

For a brighter shoeshine, place a few drops of lemon juice on your shoes when you are polishing them. Lemon juice is also great for cleaning: A small amount mixed with salt will remove mold and mildew from most surfaces. The juice is just acidic enough to do the job.

The Service's Secret to Shiny Boots

You may have heard of cadets learning how to "spit and polish" their boots, and the phrase is no colloquialism! Spit is the perfect amount of liquid to add to a large dab of polish at the toe of a boot. (Or if that's not your thing, you can simply add a bit of water.) When rubbing polish onto your boot or shoe, add a tiny bit of liquid when the polish feels rough under your rag. As you add more layers of polish, decrease the amount of spit.

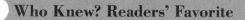

Shining your leather shoes? Forget the shoe polish. First, dampen a cloth and wipe away any dirt, then put a few drops of vegetable or olive oil on a clean, soft cloth and rub into your shoes. The oil will remove the scuff marks, and they'll shine like new. Another way to treat scuffs is by wiping them with the cut edge of a raw potato, then buffing with a soft cloth.

Give Your Leather a Pick-Me-Up

To revive the beauty of leather, lightly beat two egg whites and then apply to the leather with a soft sponge. Allow the egg whites to remain on the leather for 3–5 minutes, and then wipe off with a soft cloth dampened with clear warm water. Dry immediately and buff off any residue.

Caring for Leather Shoes

Anything made of leather requires extra love and care, and shoes are no exception. They're a big investment, but if you treat them right, you'll get the most value for your money. To wear-in new leather shoes, rub alcohol in at the heels and wear them while they're still wet. Soften them by rubbing them with olive or castor oil, which will also prevent cracking and drying.

A Facelift for Leather

Give a leather jacket a new lease on life! Mix a paste of fine white pure clay and water, adding just enough water to make a spreading consistency. Rub it into the leather, working from the bottom of the garment to the top. Leave to dry and then shake until all the clay has dropped off.

Ring Trick

If you are unable to remove a ring from your finger, run your hands under very cold water for a few seconds. The cold will make your blood vessels (and, in turn, your finger) a little bit smaller, allowing you to slip off the ring. For a really stubborn situation, go the messier route—rub baby or olive oil over the area for a little lubrication.

Remove Water from Your Watch

If you've ever seen condensation under your watch face, you know how frustrating it can be! Luckily, there's a solution. Simply strap the watch to a light bulb and turn it on for a few minutes. The heat from the bulb is the perfect amount to make the water disappear.

Prescription for Pearls

The best way to care for a pearl (or coral) necklace is to wear it regularly—oils from your skin add a gentle luster. After wearing, wipe with a chamois to remove traces of perspiration that can damage the surface.

Jewel-Polishing Potions

Wondering how to keep your beautiful jewelry looking like the first day you wore it? Follow these guidelines for the best way to polish precious and semi-precious pieces.

✦ Gentle dishwashing detergent and water plus a soft cloth can clean rubies, amethysts, citrines, sapphires, and garnets.

✦ Diamonds can be washed similarly: Fill a small pot with a cup of water, plus a teaspoon of dishwasher detergent. Add your diamonds, bring the water to a boil, then turn off the heat and let the pot sit until it cools. Once it's cool (but not before), carefully remove your jewelry and rinse.

✦ Since turquoise and opals are porous stones, never immerse them in water. Instead, polish them with a soft, dry chamois, and clean claws with a soft bristle brush.

✦ Emeralds are softer than other precious stones and can chip easily. Wash each piece by itself carefully in a warm solution of water and dishwashing liquid.

✦ Bring back the magic of marcasite by polishing it with a soft brush and then buffing with a chamois—it should never be washed.

✦ Wipe amber with a soft cloth wrung out in warm, soapy water. Dry at once (water makes amber cloudy), and wipe with sweet almond oil to remove any grease marks.

✦ Wash pearls and coral in water and very mild soap, then wipe with a soft cloth. Lay on a moist paper towel to dry.

✦ Emeralds, diamonds, rubies, and sapphires can also be washed with club soda. Place them in a glass of it overnight, and they will shine like new in the morning.

✦ Costume or inexpensive jewelry can be cleaned by dropping two Alka Seltzer tablets into a glass of water. Immerse for about five minutes and pat dry on with a clean towel.

Who Knew? Readers' Favorite

Here's an easy way to keep your earrings together: Thread the posts through old buttons, and then attach the backs.

Cork Earring Holder

Don't throw away the cork when you finish a bottle of wine. Repurpose it! Cork is a perfect material for storing and toting stud earrings. Cut the cork into thin slices, then poke the earrings through, put the backs back on, and toss them into your toiletry bag when traveling.

DIY Necklace Holders

You don't have to buy a jewelry organizer to keep your necklaces untangled. Just cut plastic straws in half, thread your necklaces through, and fasten the clasps.

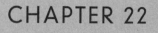
CHAPTER 22

Staying Healthy with Natural Remedies

Cheap and Easy Denture Cleanser

Here's an effective method for cleaning dentures that works just as well as the expensive tablets: Soak them overnight in a solution of 1 part white vinegar and 1 part water. The acidity of the vinegar fights tartar buildup and removes stains.

Kick Your Sweet Tooth's Habit

There are two ways to eliminate the craving for sweets (without hitting the fridge). One way is to place a small amount of salt on your tongue and let it slowly dissolve. The second: Dissolve about a teaspoon of baking soda in a glass of warm water, then rinse your mouth out and spit (don't swallow). The salt or baking soda tends to stimulate the production of saliva, which eliminates your sweet craving.

⬤ Who Knew?

When a recipe calls for vegetable oil, try substituting half of the oil with applesauce. It's an easy way to reduce the fat content in your food.

Choose Your Carbs Wisely

It's hard to resist taking something from the bread basket when you're out to eat. But if you're looking to lose weight (or just maintain it), choose a hard roll, a piece of French or Italian bread, a wafer, pita bread, or melba toast. These don't have as much butter or sugar as soft rolls, breadsticks, biscuits, croissants, and muffins.

Spice It Up for Better Health

Hot and spicy foods can help the body burn up calories. Using spices like cayenne pepper and chili powder elevates the body temperature, making the heart beat faster and requiring more energy.

Pepper Your Dishes

Why not use a sprinkling of cayenne pepper to help season your sauces? Derived from the plant *Capsicum annuum*, it has been reported to not only make you lose weight by elevating body temperature, but to improve circulation and to lower cholesterol. As it's a mild stimulant, it can also be added to hot water with lemon juice as an alternative to coffee.

Detox with Lemon

Lemon juice not only smells great, it tastes delicious, too. Mix it with hot water and try it as an alternative to hot tea and coffee. You may find it wakes you up just as well, and your body will thank you.

● Who Knew?

The body requires only a half a gram of salt daily, unless you are perspiring heavily, and the American Heart Association recommends no more than 2.4 grams of salt each day. However, the average person consumes about 6–15 grams of salt daily, which amounts to about 2 teaspoons.

Help for a Stomach Ache

If you've got an upset stomach due to indigestion or a hang-over, try drinking a glass of club soda with a dash of bitters. It should help ease your pain.

Brussels Sprouts for Wellness

Brussels sprouts are used as a general tonic for blood cleansing, as well as to cure headaches and constipation, and to reduce hardening of the arteries. Eat them regularly for good health.

Get a Feel for Fennel

Try adding fennel to roasted vegetable dishes or salads. A tasty member of the parsley family, fennel helps stabilize blood-sugar levels, thus curbing appetite. It also works to relax the muscles of the digestive system, reducing indigestion and gas pains.

A Shot of Wheatgrass

Its taste may take a tiny bit of getting used to, but a small glass of wheatgrass is packed with so many essential minerals, it's no wonder it's a hit with health food enthusiasts. Not only is it easy to grow on your own, but it contains calcium, magnesium, potassium, and iron, as well as vitamins A, B, C, and E, all of which are needed for healthy teeth, hair, and skin. Add some to your smoothie today!

Lutein for Healthy Eyes

Many people suffer from farsightedness, cataracts, glaucoma and other eye problems as they age. To keep your eyes healthy, increase your level of lutein—available in vegetables such as carrots, broccoli, spinach, Brussels sprouts and kale. Lutein can decrease the risk of cataracts and macular degeneration.

Stick with Salmon

Salmon is a great source for protein, because it contains fewer calories than many other protein sources, and it's rich in omega oils that help the development of the brain, heart, skin and joints. For the greatest health benefits, though, it's best to go for wild or organic versions.

Can the Tuna

In order to limit your mercury intake, which has been linked to brain damage in unborn babies and is thought to be toxic to adults, don't eat more than two tuna steaks or four medium-sized cans of tuna a week. Tuna, marlin, and swordfish have been found to be high in mercury deposits and should be avoided by small children, pregnant women, and women intending to become pregnant.

White Is Right

White fish is an excellent healthy food and although it isn't high in omega-3 oils, it is still a fantastic way to fill up on protein and essential minerals and amino acids without adding fat. Try halibut, skate, sea bass, and plaice as well as the usual cod and haddock.

Oil Quality Test

Olive oil is the best oil, health-wise, because it can reduce your risk of heart disease. Test the quality of your olive oil by frying a few drops in a pan—really good quality oil (which has the most health benefits) will stay green and light. If it turns dark and loses its shine, it's not as good for your health, but is still OK for sautéing.

Sugar has many names, so make sure to look closely at package labels when trying to avoid it. Here are a few of sugar's aliases: Dextrose, fructose, hexatol, high-fructose corn syrup, glucose, lactose, levulose, maltose, mannitol, sorghum, sucrose, and turbinado.

Relieve Nausea Naturally

Nothing's worse than a bad bout of nausea. Try this simple trick to help relieve your discomfort: Drink a little ginger ale, then chew a handful of crushed ice, and finally sniff a piece of black-and-white newspaper. It may seem like an old wives' tale, but it works!

Ease Bruises with a Banana

Bananas to the rescue! A simple way to help bruises fade fast is with a banana peel. Just apply a piece of banana peel, flesh side down, to the bruise, cover with a bandage, and leave on overnight. By the morning, the bruise will have faded.

Another Bruise Cure

White vinegar will also help heal bruises. Soak a cotton ball in vinegar, then apply it to the bruise for an hour. It will reduce the blueness of the bruise and speed up the healing process.

Aid Arthritis with Oatmeal

Believe it or not, you can help relieve arthritis pain with oatmeal. Just mix 2 cups oatmeal with 1 cup water, warm the mixture in the microwave, and apply to the affected area.

Guard Against Hair Loss

Thinning hair that falls out in clumps can come about as a result of a restricted diet. Hair loss from lack of vitamins B and C and iron can be rectified with a diet rich in protein and vegetables. Packed with EFAs (essential fatty acids), flax seeds will make hair thicker and shinier. If your hair has become weaker and more brittle with a tendency to break easily, try infusing rosemary in water and pour it over your hair after your final rinse. You can also massage some rosemary essential oil (mixed with baby oil) onto your scalp to help promote growth and strength.

Seaweed Wonder

To improve the thickness and condition of your hair, take a daily sea kelp supplement. This broadly found seaweed comes in several varieties but all are rich in the minerals potassium, calcium, magnesium, and iron.

Nod Off Naturally

The herb valerian has been used in traditional sleep remedies for hundreds of years. Sometimes called "valerian root," it relieves anxiety and aids the induction of sleep in a natural and non-addictive way.

Salt Sedation

If you're having trouble sleeping, but wary of popping a pill, try this instead: At bedtime drink a glass of water, then let a pinch of salt dissolve on your tongue. (Just make sure the salt doesn't touch the roof of your mouth). Studies show the combination of salt and water can induce a deep sleep.

Rejuvenate with C

Known as ascorbic acid, vitamin C is vital for collagen production, and as a powerful antioxidant it destroys harmful free radicals that cause premature aging. Best yet, this multitasking vitamin reaches every cell in the body.

A+ for Vitamin A

Vitamin A is a true wonder vitamin. Not only can it soothe and rejuvenate the skin, but it may actually be able to prevent sun damage. Liver, sweet potato, carrots, mangoes, spinach, and milk are all great sources of Vitamin A.

The All-Natural Prozac

The herbal supplement St. John's Wort can help ease feelings of depression and lift black moods. It is thought to increase the activity and prolong the action of the neurotransmitters serotonin and noradrenalin in a similar way to standard antidepressants, and will need to be taken for a few weeks before it starts working.

Stay Calm!

The most useful vitamin for healthy skin, vitamin A has the ability to calm red and blotchy skin and is also thought to visibly reduce lines and wrinkles.

Fight Stress with Pillow Pressure

Reduce stress and tension by resting on a thermal neck pillow that can be heated up in the microwave. Heat generated by the pillow penetrates into your tense neck muscles, soothing away aches and pains and relieving headaches and those oh-so-aging frowns.

Pinch to Relieve Stress

Many people hold stress in the area between their eyebrows, and in time, vertical stress lines will develop here. When you feel your brow knit together with concentration or stress, take a moment to pinch the muscle there, working from the center of the brow along the brow-line in each direction with a thumb and bent forefinger. Not only will it make you feel better, it will prevent wrinkles, too!

Essential Oils

The right essential oils can help to relieve tension and de-stress. Try lavender, chamomile, geranium, spearmint, or peppermint. Add these delicious-smelling oils to your bath water for a relaxing soak, or inhale them by placing a few drops on a cotton pad.

Suffering from Sunburn?

Nothing's worse than a bad sunburn. The good news is you don't need an expensive lotion to soothe your poor, burnt skin. Just cut an apple in half, remove the core, and rub over the affected area for 3–4 minutes. Apples will keep your skin from blistering or peeling.

Rash Soother

An effective and natural way to soothe diaper rash is by adding a cup of baking soda to your baby's bathwater.

As Nice as Ice

The next time you need a quick ice pack, just grab a bag of frozen vegetables from your freezer. It does the trick, and won't leak like a bag filled with ice cubes.

Rough-and-Ready Hot Packs

In an emergency, a one-liter plastic soda bottle can make an excellent hot-water bottle. Just make sure that you wrap it in a hand towel before placing it against your skin.

Who Knew? Readers' Favorite

The easiest way to remove a splinter? Just put a drop of white glue over the offending piece of wood, let it dry, and then peel off the dried glue. The splinter will stick to the glue and come right out.

Rx, Vinegar

White vinegar stops nosebleeds. Just dampen a cotton ball and plug the nostril. The acetic acid in the vinegar cauterizes the wound. Who knew?

Index

A

aerosol cooking sprays, 256
aerosol oven cleaners, 35
    air fresheners, homemade, 32–33
    fabric softener, 18
    oranges, 17
    vanilla, 17
all-purpose cleaner, 37
aluminum foil
    and food, 132
    and pets, 15
ammonia, 37
anchovies, 183
apples, 275
    baked, 276
arthritis, oatmeal for, 317
artwork, 12
automobiles. See cars
avocados, 150, 274

B

baby wipes, 76
bacon
    spattering, reduction of, 159–60
    storage, 160
baked sales, 241
baking, 196, 231
    baking dishes, and rust, 278
    biscuits, 239–40
    blending, 234
    butter and margarine, 207
    clean-up, 241
    cupcakes and muffins, 233–34, 238
    dried fruits, 236
    electric stand mixers, 231
    freezing, 244
    greased and floured pans, 232–33
    muffins, removal from pan, 238
baking powder, 137, 241
baking soda
    and coffee, 264
    on carpet stains, 20
    to clean coffee makers, 35
    in milk, 257
    potency of, 137
    with vegetables, 148
    for water stains, 14
bananas, 255
    for bruises, 316
    as popsicles, 202–3
barbecue sauce, 223
barbecues, 221–229. See also grilling
baseball caps, cleaning, 304
bathroom, 46–54
    ambience in, 54
    bar soap, 52
    bathroom window "frost," 53
    ceramic tile, 50
    chrome and glass, 47–48, 50
    cleaning of, 47, 51
    copper stains, 48
    defogging glass, 54
    drawers, 53
    electrical appliance cords, 54
    grout, 51
    hair spray, 51
    mildew removal, 47, 49
    mirrors, 48
    porcelain, 50
    shower curtains, 50
    shower doors, 49
    shower heads, 47–48
    soap scum, 49
    toilet bowl cleaner, 49
    toothbrushes, 53
baths
    bubble bath, 294–95
    bath oil, 295
batteries, 29, 78
beans, 190–91
    baked, 162
beauty, 281–298
bedrooms, 69–78
    closet doors, 71
    drapes and bedspreads, 71
    dresser drawers, 72–73
    headboards, 70
    mattresses, 71
    pillows, 71
    radiators, energy savers, 71
    storage space in, 72
beer, 13, 229
beets, 193

C